At Issue

Is There a New Cold War?

Other Books in the At Issue Series:

At Issue

Is There a New Cold War?

Stefan Kiesbye, Book Editor

GREENHAVEN PRESS
A part of Gale, Cengage Learning

GALE
CENGAGE Learning™

Detroit • New York • San Francisco • New Haven, Conn • Waterville, Maine • London

Christine Nasso, *Publisher*
Elizabeth Des Chenes, *Managing Editor*

© 2010 Greenhaven Press, a part of Gale, Cengage Learning.

Gale and Greenhaven Press are registered trademarks used herein under license.

For more information, contact:
Greenhaven Press
27500 Drake Rd.
Farmington Hills, MI 48331-3535
Or you can visit our Internet site at gale.cengage.com

Cover image © Images.com/Corbis

LIBRARY OF CONGRESS CATALOGING-IN-PUBLICATION DATA

Is there a new Cold War? / Stefan Kiesbye, book editor.
   p. cm. -- (At issue)
  Includes bibliographical references and index.
  ISBN 978-0-7377-4659-4 (hardcover) -- ISBN 978-0-7377-4660-0 (pbk.)
  1. United States--Foreign relations--Russia (Federation) 2. Russia (Federation)--Foreign relations--United States. 3. United States--Military policy. 4. United States--Foreign relations--2001-2009. 5. United States--Foreign relations--2009-. 6. Russia (Federation)--Military policy. 7. Russia (Federation)--Foreign relations. 8. World politics--2005-2015. 9. International relations. 10. Security, International. I. Kiesbye, Stefan.
  E183.8.R9I8 2010
  327.47073--dc22
                                            2009037780

Printed in the United States of America
1 2 3 4 5 6 7 14 13 12 11 10

Contents

Introduction

During the Cold War (1945–1991), the United States of America and the Soviet Union sought to expand their spheres of influence around the world or keep each other from doing so. One clear example of this rivalry is the Soviet Union's early dealings, and later conflict, with Afghanistan. According to scholar Michael Rubin, already in the mid-1950s "[B]oth the Soviet Union and the United States increasingly plied Afghanistan with economic and technical assistance. [The Afghani] government sought to buy arms, and approached the United States several times between 1953 and 1955. However [it] was unable to come to an agreement with Washington, which tied arms sales to either membership in the anti-Communist Baghdad Pact or at least in a Mutual Security Pact. The Soviet Union, though, was eager to supply what the United States would not. In 1956, Afghanistan purchased $25 million in tanks, airplanes, helicopters, and small arms from the Soviet bloc, while Soviet experts helped construct or convert to military specifications airfields in northern Afghanistan. The Cold War had come to Afghanistan."

In 1979, the Afghani Communist regime faced internal opposition, and as armed conflicts escalated, the Soviet Union deployed troops to Afghanistan at the request of the Afghani government. The United States took the side of the anti-Communist rebels, and covertly supported their efforts. Zbigniew Brzezinski, National Security Advisor to President Jimmy Carter, stated in an interview years after the conflict, "[w]e didn't push the Russians to intervene, but we knowingly increased the probability that they would . . . That secret operation was an excellent idea. It had the effect of drawing the Soviets into the Afghan trap . . . The day that the Soviets officially crossed the border, I wrote to President Carter. We now have the opportunity of giving to the Soviet Union its Vietnam War."

By the mid-1980s, the resistance to Soviet forces received military help from the United States, Saudi Arabia, Pakistan, China, and Great Britain. Foreign fighters from other Muslim countries joined the effort, among them Osama bin Laden. In 1985, President Ronald Reagan decided to provide the Mujahideen Stingers with anti-aircraft missiles, openly breaking an embargo on American arms. By 1987 the Soviets had almost completely stopped their offensive against the Afghanis and prepared to withdraw from the region.

The Soviet Union withdrew the last of its troops from Afghanistan in February of 1989, having suffered heavy casualties throughout the unpopular conflict. That same year the Berlin Wall was demolished and Communist governments were toppled in Bulgaria, Romania, and Czechoslovakia; the Soviet Union fell into decline as communism was challenged. The Cold War officially ended with the formal dissolution of the Soviet Union in 1991. Commentators disagree on what impact, if any, the Afghanistan conflict had on the Soviet Union's collapse.

Today, talk of a new cold war circulates in the newspapers and on Web sites. Unlike in the decades immediately following World War II, when the Cold War between the United States and the Soviet Union played out, it's not quite clear who the new players are. As fractured as the political world seemed during the time of the Afghan-Soviet War, the USSR and the United States were always the major forces, the only two superpowers. Now many contend that not only is Russia reemerging as a veritable force, but other countries are also vying for power. China is ready to make its political and economic influence felt. Large and small nations have acquired and tested nuclear bombs, and totalitarian regimes such as North Korea seem to threaten global security. Iran is seeking to expand its nuclear program, and its strained relations with the Western World worry many analysts. And finally, the European Union has established itself as an economic and political powerhouse. In the following essays, analysts debate whether a new cold war is beginning and if this new war could pitch America against new or old foes.

1

There Is a New Cold War

Stephen Cohen

Stephen Cohen, professor of Russian studies at New York University, is the author (with Katrina vanden Heuvel) of Voices of Glasnost: Conversations With Gorbachev's Reformers *and* Failed Crusade: America and the Tragedy of Post-Communist Russia.

Since the collapse of the Soviet Union, American foreign policy has failed to respond effectively to the changing political landscape of Russia and its neighbors. Instead of seeking to stabilize a nation in crisis, the United States has taken advantage of its former enemy to expand NATO and gain political influence in neighboring countries. While condemning Russia for democratic shortcomings and military escapades, the George W. Bush administration pushed its missile defense system and reheated a nuclear and conventional arms race.

Contrary to established opinion, the gravest threats to America's national security are still in Russia. They derive from an unprecedented development that most US policymakers have recklessly disregarded, as evidenced by the undeclared cold war Washington has waged, under both parties, against post-Communist Russia during the past fifteen years.

As a result of the Soviet breakup in 1991, Russia, a state bearing every nuclear and other device of mass destruction, virtually collapsed. During the 1990s its essential infrastructures—political, economic and social—disintegrated. Moscow's hold on its vast territories was weakened by separatism, official corruption and Mafia-like crime. The worst peacetime depression in modern history brought economic losses more than twice those suffered in World War II. GDP [gross domestic product] plummeted by nearly half and capital investment by 80 percent. Most Russians were thrown into poverty. Death rates soared and the population shrank. And in August 1998, the financial system imploded.

No one in authority anywhere had ever foreseen that one of the twentieth century's two superpowers would plunge, along with its arsenals of destruction, into such catastrophic circumstances. Even today, we cannot be sure what Russia's collapse might mean for the rest of the world.

A Fragile Economy

Outwardly, the nation may now seem to have recovered. Its economy has grown on average by 6 to 7 percent annually since 1999, its stock-market index increased last year [2005] by 83 percent and its gold and foreign currency reserves are the world's fifth largest. Moscow is booming with new construction, frenzied consumption of Western luxury goods and fifty-six large casinos. Some of this wealth has trickled down to the provinces and middle and lower classes, whose income has been rising. But these advances, loudly touted by the Russian government and Western investment-fund promoters, are due largely to high world prices for the country's oil and gas and stand out only in comparison with the wasteland of 1998.

More fundamental realities indicate that Russia remains in an unprecedented state of peacetime demodernization and depopulation. Investment in the economy and other basic infrastructures remains barely a third of the 1990 level. Some two-thirds of Russians still live below or very near the poverty line, including 80 percent of families with two or more children, 60 percent of rural citizens and large segments of the educated and professional classes, among them teachers, doctors and military officers. The gap between the poor and the rich, Russian experts tell us, is becoming "explosive."

Most tragic and telling, the nation continues to suffer wartime death and birth rates, its population declining by 700,000 or more every year. Male life expectancy is barely 59 years and, at the other end of the life cycle, 2 to 3 million children are homeless. Old and new diseases, from tuberculosis to HIV infections, have grown into epidemics. Nationalists may exaggerate in charging that "the Motherland is dying," but even the head of Moscow's most pro-Western university warns that Russia remains in "extremely deep crisis."

A One-Man Government

The stability of the political regime atop this bleak post-Soviet landscape rests heavily, if not entirely, on the personal popularity and authority of one man, [former] President Vladimir Putin, who admits the state "is not yet completely stable." While Putin's ratings are an extraordinary 70 to 75 percent positive, political institutions and would-be leaders below him have almost no public support.

The top business and administrative elites, having rapaciously "privatized" the Soviet state's richest assets in the 1990s, are particularly despised. Indeed, their possession of that property, because it lacks popular legitimacy, remains a time bomb embedded in the political and economic system. The huge military is equally unstable, its ranks torn by a lack of funds, abuses of authority and discontent. No wonder serious analysts worry that one or more sudden developments—a sharp fall in world oil prices, more major episodes of ethnic violence or terrorism or Putin's disappearance—might plunge Russia into an even worse crisis. Pointing to the disorder spreading from Chechnya through the country's southern rim, for example, the eminent scholar Peter Reddaway even asks "whether Russia is stable enough to hold together."

As long as catastrophic possibilities exist in that nation, so do the unprecedented threats to US and international security. Experts differ as to which danger is the gravest—proliferation of Russia's enormous stockpile of nuclear, chemical and biological materials; ill-maintained nuclear reactors on land and on decommissioned submarines; an impaired early-warning system controlling missiles on hair-trigger alert; or the first-ever civil war in a shattered superpower, the terror-ridden Chechen conflict. But no one should doubt that together they constitute a much greater constant threat than any the United States faced during the Soviet era.

The real US policy has been . . . a relentless, winner-take-all exploitation of Russia's post-1991 weakness.

Nor is a catastrophe involving weapons of mass destruction the only danger in what remains the world's largest territorial country. Nearly a quarter of the planet's people live on Russia's borders, among them conflicting ethnic and religious groups. Any instability in Russia could easily spread to a crucial and exceedingly volatile part of the world. . . .

Failed Strategies

Since the early 1990s Washington has simultaneously conducted, under Democrats and Republicans, two fundamentally different policies toward post-Soviet Russia—one decorative and outwardly reassuring, the other real and exceedingly reckless. The decorative policy, which has been taken at face value in the United States, at least until recently, professes to have replaced America's previous cold war intentions with a generous relationship of "strategic partnership and friendship." The public image of this approach has featured happy-talk meetings between American and Russian presidents, first "Bill and Boris" (Clinton and Yeltsin), then "George and Vladimir" (Bush and Putin).

The real US policy has been very different—a relentless, winner-take-all exploitation of Russia's post-1991 weakness. Accompanied by broken American promises, condescending lectures and demands for unilateral concessions, it has been even more aggressive and uncompromising than was Washington's approach to Soviet Communist Russia. Consider its defining elements as they have unfolded—with fulsome support in both American political parties, influential newspapers and policy think tanks—since the early 1990s:

A growing military encirclement of Russia, on and near its borders, by US and NATO [North Atlantic Treaty Organization] bases, which are already ensconced or being planned in at least half the fourteen other former Soviet republics, from the Baltics and Ukraine to Georgia, Azerbaijan and the new states of Central Asia. The result is a US-built reverse iron curtain and the remilitarization of American-Russian relations.

When Washington meddles in the politics of Georgia and Ukraine, it is "promoting democracy"; when the Kremlin does so, it is "neoimperialism."

A tacit (and closely related) US denial that Russia has any legitimate national interests outside its own territory, even in ethnically akin or contiguous former republics such as Ukraine, Belarus and Georgia. How else to explain, to take a bellwether example, the thinking of Richard Holbrooke, Democratic would-be Secretary of State? While roundly condemning the Kremlin for promoting a pro-Moscow government in neighboring Ukraine, where Russia has centuries of shared linguistic, marital, religious, economic and security ties, Holbrooke declares that far-away Slav nation part of "our core zone of security."

Even more, a presumption that Russia does not have full sovereignty within its own borders, as expressed by constant

US interventions in Moscow's internal affairs since 1992. They have included an on-site crusade by swarms of American "advisers," particularly during the 1990s, to direct Russia's "transition" from Communism; endless missionary sermons from afar, often couched in threats, on how that nation should and should not organize its political and economic systems; and active support for Russian anti-Kremlin groups, some associated with hated Yeltsin-era oligarchs.

Dangerous Meddling

That interventionary impulse has now grown even into suggestions that Putin be overthrown by the kind of US-backed "color revolutions" carried out since 2003 in Georgia, Ukraine and Kyrgyzstan, and attempted this year [2006] in Belarus. Thus, while mainstream editorial pages increasingly call the Russian president "thug," "fascist" and "Saddam Hussein," one of the Carnegie Endowment's several Washington crusaders assures us of "Putin's weakness" and vulnerability to "regime change." (Do proponents of "democratic regime change" in Russia care that it might mean destabilizing a nuclear state?)

Underpinning these components of the real US policy are familiar cold war double standards condemning Moscow for doing what Washington does—such as seeking allies and military bases in former Soviet republics, using its assets (oil and gas in Russia's case) as aid to friendly governments and regulating foreign money in its political life.

The cold war ended in Moscow, but not in Washington, as is clear from a brief look back.

More broadly, when NATO expands to Russia's front and back doorsteps, gobbling up former Soviet-bloc members and republics, it is "fighting terrorism" and "protecting new states"; when Moscow protests, it is engaging in "cold war thinking." When Washington meddles in the politics of Georgia and

Ukraine, it is "promoting democracy"; when the Kremlin does so, it is "neoimperialism." And not to forget the historical background: When in the 1990s the US-supported Yeltsin overthrew Russia's elected Parliament and Constitutional Court by force, gave its national wealth and television networks to Kremlin insiders, imposed a constitution without real constraints on executive power and rigged elections, it was "democratic reform"; when Putin continues that process, it is "authoritarianism."

Finally, the United States is attempting, by exploiting Russia's weakness, to acquire the nuclear superiority it could not achieve during the Soviet era. That is the essential meaning of two major steps taken by the Bush Administration in 2002, both against Moscow's strong wishes. One was the Administration's unilateral withdrawal from the 1972 Anti-Ballistic Missile Treaty, freeing it to try to create a system capable of destroying incoming missiles and thereby the capacity to launch a nuclear first strike without fear of retaliation. The other was pressuring the Kremlin to sign an ultimately empty nuclear weapons reduction agreement requiring no actual destruction of weapons and indeed allowing development of new ones; providing for no verification; and permitting unilateral withdrawal before the specified reductions are required.

Washington's Cold War

The extraordinarily anti-Russian nature of these policies casts serious doubt on two American official and media axioms: that the recent "chill" in US-Russian relations has been caused by Putin's behavior at home and abroad, and that the cold war ended fifteen years ago. The first axiom is false, the second only half true: The cold war ended in Moscow, but not in Washington, as is clear from a brief look back.

The last Soviet leader, Mikhail Gorbachev, came to power in 1985 with heretical "New Thinking" that proposed not merely to ease but to actually abolish the decades-long cold war. His proposals triggered a fateful struggle in Washington (and Moscow) between policy-makers who wanted to seize the historic opportunity and those who did not. President Ronald Reagan decided to meet Gorbachev at least part of the way, as did his successor, the first President George Bush. As a result, in December 1989, at a historic summit meeting at Malta, Gorbachev and Bush declared the cold war over. (That extraordinary agreement evidently has been forgotten; thus we have the *New York Times* recently asserting that the US-Russian relationship today "is far better than it was 15 years ago.")

Declarations alone, however, could not terminate decades of warfare attitudes. Even when [George H.W.] Bush was agreeing to end the cold war in 1989–91, many of his top advisers, like many members of the US political elite and media, strongly resisted. (I witnessed that rift on the eve of Malta, when I was asked to debate the issue in front of Bush and his divided foreign policy team.) Proof came with the Soviet breakup in December 1991: US officials and the media immediately presented the purported "end of the cold war" not as a mutual Soviet-American decision, which it certainly was, but as a great American victory and Russian defeat.

Ill-Advised Foreign Policy

That (now standard) triumphalist narrative is the primary reason the cold war was quickly revived—not in Moscow a decade later by Putin but in Washington in the early 1990s, when the Clinton Administration made two epically unwise decisions. One was to treat post-Communist Russia as a defeated nation that was expected to replicate America's domestic practices and bow to its foreign policies. It required, behind the facade of the Clinton-Yeltsin "partnership and friendship" (as Clinton's top "Russia hand," Strobe Talbott, later confirmed), telling Yeltsin "here's some more shit for your face" and Moscow's "submissiveness." From that triumphalism grew the still-ongoing interventions in Moscow's internal affairs and the abiding notion that Russia has no autonomous rights at home or abroad. . . .

For its part, the [George W. Bush] White House deleted from its 2006 National Security Strategy the long-professed US-Russian partnership, backtracked on agreements to help Moscow join the World Trade Organization and adopted sanctions against Belarus, the Slav former republic most culturally akin to Russia and with whom the Kremlin is negotiating a new union state. Most significant, in May [2006] it dispatched Vice President [Dick] Cheney to an anti-Russian conference in former Soviet Lithuania, now a NATO member, to denounce the Kremlin and make clear it is not "a strategic partner and a trusted friend," thereby ending fifteen years of official pretense.

American Double Standards

More astonishing is a Council on Foreign Relations "task force report" on Russia, co-chaired by Democratic [2008] presidential [election] aspirant John Edwards, issued in March [2006]. The "nonpartisan" council's reputed moderation and balance are nowhere in evidence. An unrelenting exercise in double standards, the report blames all the "disappointments" in US-Russian relations solely on "Russia's wrong direction" under Putin—from meddling in the former Soviet republics and backing Iran to conflicts over NATO, energy politics and the "rollback of Russian democracy."

Strongly implying that Bush has been too soft on Putin, the council report flatly rejects partnership with Moscow as "not a realistic prospect." It calls instead for "selective cooperation" and "selective opposition," depending on which suits US interests, and, in effect, Soviet-era containment. Urging more Western intervention in Moscow's political affairs, the report even reserves for Washington the right to reject Russia's future elections and leaders as "illegitimate." An article in the council's influential journal *Foreign Affairs* menacingly adds that the United States is quickly "attaining nuclear primacy" and the ability "to destroy the long-range nuclear arsenals of Russia or China with a first strike."

Every consequence of this bipartisan American cold war against post-Communist Russia has exacerbated the dangers inherent in the Soviet breakup mentioned above. The crusade to transform Russia during the 1990s, with its disastrous "shock therapy" economic measures and resulting antidemocratic acts, further destabilized the country, fostering an oligarchical system that plundered the state's wealth, deprived essential infrastructures of investment, impoverished the people and nurtured dangerous corruption. In the process, it discredited Western-style reform, generated mass anti-Americanism where there had been almost none—only 5 percent of Russians surveyed in May [2006] thought the United States was a "friend"—and eviscerated the once-influential pro-American faction in Kremlin and electoral politics.

Military encirclement, the [George W.] Bush Administration's striving for nuclear supremacy and today's renewed US intrusions into Russian politics are having even worse consequences. They have provoked the Kremlin into undertaking its own conventional and nuclear buildup, relying more rather than less on compromised mechanisms of control and maintenance, while continuing to invest miserly sums in the country's decaying economic base and human resources. The same American policies have also caused Moscow to cooperate less rather than more in existing US-funded programs to reduce the multiple risks represented by Russia's materials of mass destruction and to prevent accidental nuclear war. More generally, they have inspired a new Kremlin ideology of "emphasizing our sovereignty" that is increasingly nationalistic, intolerant of foreign-funded NGOs [nongovernmental organizations] as "fifth columns" [groups that clandestinely undermine other groups, in this case the Russian government] and reliant on anti-Western views of the "patriotic" Russian intelligentsia and the Orthodox Church. . . .

Certainly, nothing Moscow has gotten from Washington since 1992 . . . "compensates for the geopolitical harm the United States is doing to Russia."

Moscow's Reaction Against the U.S. Could Be Dangerous

In the US-Russian struggle in Central Asia over Caspian oil and gas, Washington, as even the triumphalist Thomas Friedman admits, "is at a severe disadvantage." The United States has already lost its military base in Uzbekistan and may soon lose the only remaining one in the region, in Kyrgyzstan; the new pipeline it backed to bypass Russia runs through Georgia, whose stability depends considerably on Moscow; Washington's new friend in oil-rich Azerbaijan is an anachronistic dynastic ruler; and Kazakhstan, whose enormous energy reserves make it a particular US target, has its own large Russian population and is moving back toward Moscow.

Nor is the Kremlin powerless in direct dealings with the West. It can mount more than enough warheads to defeat any missile shield and illusion of "nuclear primacy." It can shut US businesses out of multibillion-dollar deals in Russia and, as it recently reminded the European Union, which gets 25 percent of its gas from Russia, "redirect supplies" to hungry markets in the East. And Moscow could deploy its resources, connections and UN Security Council veto against US interests involving, for instance, nuclear proliferation, Iran, Afghanistan and possibly even Iraq.

Contrary to exaggerated US accusations, the Kremlin has not yet resorted to such retaliatory measures in any significant way. But unless Washington stops abasing and encroaching on

Russia, there is no "sovereign" reason why it should not do so. Certainly, nothing Moscow has gotten from Washington since 1992, a Western security specialist emphasizes, "compensates for the geopolitical harm the United States is doing to Russia."

A Thirst for Oil

American crusaders insist it is worth the risk in order to democratize Russia and other former Soviet republics. In reality, their campaigns since 1992 have only discredited that cause in Russia. Praising the despised Yeltsin and endorsing other unpopular figures as Russia's "democrats," while denouncing the popular Putin, has associated democracy with the social pain, chaos and humiliation of the 1990s. Ostracizing Belarus President Aleksandr Lukashenko while embracing tyrants in Azerbaijan and Kazakhstan has related it to the thirst for oil. Linking "democratic revolutions" in Ukraine and Georgia to NATO membership has equated them with US expansionism. Focusing on the victimization of billionaire Mikhail Khodorkhovsky and not on Russian poverty or ongoing mass protests against social injustices has suggested democracy is only for oligarchs. And by insisting on their indispensable role, US crusaders have all but said (wrongly) that Russians are incapable of democracy or resisting abuses of power on their own.

Time for a new US policy is running out, but there is no hint of one in official or unofficial circles.

The result is dark Russian suspicions of American intentions ignored by US policy-makers and media alike. They include the belief that Washington's real purpose is to take control of the country's energy resources and nuclear weapons and use encircling NATO satellite states to "de-sovereignize" Russia, turning it into a "vassal of the West." More generally, US policy has fostered the belief that the American cold war was never really aimed at Soviet Communism but always at

Russia, a suspicion given credence by *Post* and *Times* columnists who characterize Russia even after Communism as an inherently "autocratic state" with "brutish instincts."

To overcome those towering obstacles to a new relationship, Washington has to abandon the triumphalist conceits primarily responsible for the revived cold war and its growing dangers. It means respecting Russia's sovereign right to determine its course at home (including disposal of its energy resources). As the record plainly shows, interfering in Moscow's internal affairs, whether on-site or from afar, only harms the chances for political liberties and economic prosperity that still exist in that tormented nation.

It also means acknowledging Russia's legitimate security interests, especially in its own "near abroad." In particular, the planned third expansion of NATO, intended to include Ukraine, must not take place. Extending NATO to Russia's doorsteps has already brought relations near the breaking point (without actually benefiting any nation's security); absorbing Ukraine, which Moscow regards as essential to its Slavic identity and its military defense, may be the point of no return, as even pro-US Russians anxiously warn. Nor would it be democratic, since nearly two-thirds of Ukrainians are opposed. The explosive possibilities were adumbrated in late May and early June [2006] when local citizens in ethnic Russian Crimea blockaded a port and roads where a US naval ship and contingent of Marines suddenly appeared, provoking resolutions declaring the region "anti-NATO territory" and threats of "a new Vietnam."

New Policies Are Needed

Time for a new US policy is running out, but there is no hint of one in official or unofficial circles. Denouncing the Kremlin in May [2006], Cheney spoke "like a triumphant cold warrior," a *Times* correspondent reported. A top State Department official has already announced the "next great mission" in and around Russia. In the same unreconstructed spirit, [former Secretary of State Condoleezza] Rice has demanded Russians "recognize that we have legitimate interests . . . in their neighborhood," without a word about Moscow's interests; and a former Clinton official has held the Kremlin "accountable for the ominous security threats . . . developing between NATO's eastern border and Russia." Meanwhile, the [George W.] Bush Administration is playing Russian roulette with Moscow's control of its nuclear weapons. Its missile shield project having already provoked a destabilizing Russian buildup, the Administration now proposes to further confuse Moscow's early-warning system, risking an accidental launch, by putting conventional warheads on long-range missiles for the first time.

In a democracy we might expect alternative policy proposals from would-be leaders. But there are none in either party, only demands for a more anti-Russian course, or silence. We should not be surprised. Acquiescence in [George W.] Bush's monstrous war in Iraq has amply demonstrated the political elite's limited capacity for introspection, independent thought and civic courage. (It prefers to falsely blame the American people, as the managing editor of *Foreign Affairs* recently did, for craving "ideological red meat.") It may also be intimidated by another revived cold war practice—personal defamation. The *Post* and *The New Yorker* have already labeled critics of their Russia policy "Putin apologists" and charged them with "appeasement" and "again taking the Russian side of the Cold War."

The vision and courage of heresy will therefore be needed to escape today's new cold war orthodoxies and dangers, but it is hard to imagine a US politician answering the call. There is, however, a not-too-distant precedent. Twenty years ago, when the world faced exceedingly grave cold war perils, Gorbachev unexpectedly emerged from the orthodox and repres-

2

The New Cold War Is a Myth

Stephen Kotkin

Stephen Kotkin is a professor of history and director of the Program in Russian Studies at Princeton University.

It is false to believe that Russia was on its way to becoming a democracy under Boris Yeltsin, and that the country plunged into a renewed dictatorship once Vladimir Putin came to power.

To see and describe Russia in American terms is a failure to understand the particularities of a country that has a thriving market economy, yet does not open itself to democracy. Russia is no new menace to the world, partly because its economy isn't strong enough to support a new cold war and an accompanying arms race.

What is it about Russia that drives the Anglo-American world mad? Soviet communism collapses, the empire is relinquished. Then come the wild hopes and failures of the 1990s—including the 1993 half-coup and the tank assault on Russia's legislature, the results-adjusted referendum on a new constitution (still in force), the dubious privatisations, the war in Chechnya and the financial default in 1998. But after all that, in December 1999 Boris Yeltsin apologises, steps down early—and names his prime minister and former secret police [KGB] chief Vladimir Putin as acting president. To widespread consternation, Yeltsin predicts that the obscure spy is the man to "unite around himself those who will revive Great Russia." Incredibly, this is exactly what transpires.

And this is a grand disappointment, even a frightening prospect? The elevation of Putin—a secret deal promoted by Yeltsin's personal and political family, motivated less by patriotism than self-preservation—will go down as one of the most enduring aspects of Yeltsin's shaky legacy. Now, Putin, just like his benefactor, has selected his successor, Russia's new president Dmitri Medvedev. Sure, Putin has no plans to retire to a hospital-dacha, where Yeltsin had spent much of his presidency. Still, in his crafty way Putin has abided by the constitutional limit of two presidential terms. In May [2008], Medvedev will acquire the immense powers of the Russian presidency (a gift of Yeltsin) in circumstances whereby the Russian state is no longer incoherent (a gift of Putin). And this is grounds for near universal dismissal in the West?

Two Myths Blur the Picture

Two clashing myths have opened a gulf of misunderstanding towards Russia. First is the myth in the West that the chaos and impoverishment under Yeltsin amounted to a rough democracy, which Putin went on to destroy. When something comes undone that easily, it was probably never what it was cracked up to be. Still, the myth of Russia's overturned democracy unites cold war nostalgists, who miss the enemy, with a new generation of Russia-watchers, many of whom participated earnestly in the illusory 1990s democracy-building project in Russia and are now disillusioned (and tenured).

Even though many Russian officials are conscientious and competent, the state remains too corrupt, as in most places around the world.

Second is the myth, on the Russian side, that the KGB was the one Soviet-era institution that was uncorrupted, patriotic and able to restore order. This credits Putin's stooge entourage for the economic liberalisation that was actually pushed through by the non-KGB personnel around him.

Each of these myths deeply rankles the other side. When a big majority of Russians accept or even applaud Putin's concentration of power, Anglo-American observers suspect not just ignorance but a love of authoritarianism. (Unfortunately, Russians have never been offered genuine democracy and the rule of law alongside soaring living standards.) When foreign-based commentators and academics celebrate Yeltsin's Russia, which was worth a paltry $200bn [billion] and suffered international humiliation, while denouncing Putin's Russia, which has a GDP of $1.3 trillion and has regained global stature, most Russians detect not just incomprehension but ill-will.

For the most part, pathetic cries about how "the West," whatever that is, has (again) "lost" Russia, and how the West must somehow "resist" Putin, persist.

Let's take a deep breath. To recognise that Putin inherited a dysfunctional situation derived from rampant insider theft and regional misrule is not to condone his KGB-style rule, which has often been nasty and sometimes self-defeating. Even though many Russian officials are conscientious and competent, the state remains too corrupt, as in most places around the world. At the top, privileged functionaries have grabbed (and are still grabbing) prime business holdings. At all levels, officialdom now seeks its rewards by mimicking the Kremlin's repression and manipulation. But Russia is also increasingly prosperous, with a new consumer-driven market economy and a burgeoning middle-class society full of pride. This combination of a relatively closed, unstable political system and a relatively open, stable society may seem incompatible—but there it is.

What happens when a large, important country turns out to have a dynamic, open market economy integrated into the global system, yet a political system that is undemocratic and not democratising? A lot of head-scratching by experts. It may be comforting in the corridors of punditry and social science to write about how economic growth without the rule of law is doomed to fail (China?) or how economic growth eventually brings political liberalisation. But many countries, not just Russia, have more or less manipulated elections while lacking the rule of law, and yet still have dynamic market economies. In Russia private property is not guaranteed—and property ownership is widespread.

In the US, Russia's very make-up, let alone its conduct, is treated as nothing less than an issue of American identity.

A Market Revolution

A conceptual adjustment to Russia's seemingly impossible reality is now under way, but the process is painful and slow. "When I worked in Moscow in 1994 and 1995 for the National Democratic Institute, an American NGO [nongovernmental organization], I could not have imagined the present situation," confessed Sarah Mendelson, a senior fellow in Russian affairs at the Centre for Strategic and International Studies, in the *American Scholar* recently. "We thought we were on the frontier of a democratic revolution. We weren't. We were witnessing a market revolution." This basic understanding, so long in coming, is not yet widespread. For the most part, pathetic cries about how "the West," whatever that is, has (again) "lost" Russia, and how the West must somehow "resist" Putin, persist.

Edward Lucas, by his telling, was once deported by the KGB. This happened in 1990, when Lucas, a British passport-holder, entered Lithuania on a Lithuanian visa after it declared its independence but before the Soviet Union had been formally dissolved. As far as this reviewer is aware, Lucas has never been imprisoned for his convictions. Still, though not technically a dissident, he argues like one. That is how a very perspicacious [discerning] journalist like Lucas, the central and eastern Europe correspondent of the *Economist*, could end up writing a not very persuasive polemic called "The New Cold War: How the Kremlin Menaces Both Russia and the West." Russia, he argues, is aggressively waging a global war for influence with its vast natural resources and piles of cash, and although the US and Britain are trying to stand up to the mighty bear, Germany is colluding, and China is, possibly, "co-operating." . . .

Losing Russia

"We are," Lucas himself concludes, "back in the era of great-power politics." Welcome to the 18th century. Still, there's one very important exception here. The political friars in London, Berlin and even Brussels will manage a modus vivendi [a temporary agreement between disputing parties] with Russia as well as China, while holding at home to their liberal and democratic values. But can Washington, the capital of a country that has only been around since the era of the civilising mission and ultimately owes its existence to Puritans, survive a world without self-assigned crusades? In the US, Russia's very make-up, let alone its conduct, is treated as nothing less than an issue of American identity.

Just how many times can America "lose" Russia? A limitless number, it seems. But there may be hope: someone has finally traced in compelling detail the long-standing, religiously inspired American movement to remake Russia. In *The American Mission and the "Evil Empire": The Crusade for a "Free Russia" since 1881*, David S. Foglesong, a professor at Rutgers University, shows that the missionaries, economic advisers and activists promoting God, capitalism and freedom in Russia stretch back in time to America's former slave abolitionists.

American fascination with Russia took off with the terrorists' assassination of Czar Alexander II in St. Petersburg in 1881, after which, James William Buel, a Missouri journalist and author of a popular account of the outlaws Jesse and Frank James, dashed across the tsarist empire to gather material for a book. "Civilisation is spreading rapidly eastward; it cannot stop or go around Russia," Buel wrote, "and whether with bayonet or psalm-book the march will be made through every part of the czar's dominions."

Russia's state-owned companies . . . whatever their dubious methods, have not been resting on their bureaucratic laurels but rather acquiring assets for the money (and ego).

Foglesong demonstrates that powerful Americans have again and again seen the possibility, even necessity, of spreading the word to Russia, and then, when Russia fails to transform itself into something resembling the US, have recoiled and condemned Russia's perfidious national character or its leaders—most recently Putin. The author's singular achievement is to show that well before the cold war, Russia served as America's dark double, an object of wishful thinking, condescension and self-righteousness in a quest for American purpose—without much to show for such efforts inside Russia. The author thereby places in context the cold war, when pamphleteers like William F. Buckley Jr. and politicians like Ronald Reagan pushed a crusade to revitalise the American spirit. Russia then was a threat but also a means to America's end (some fixed on a rollback of the alleged Soviet "spawn" inside the US—the welfare state—while others, after the Vietnam debacle, wanted to restore "faith in the United States as a virtuous nation with a unique historical mission"). Foglesong's exposé of Americans' "heady sense of their country's unique blessings" helps make sense of the giddiness, followed by rank disillusionment, vis-à-vis the post-Soviet Russia of the 1990s and 2000s.

The U.S. Efforts to Cooperate with Russia

In today's downer phase of the recurrent cycle that Foglesong identifies, however, the mission endures. Consider that, in 2006, Stephen Sestanovich of the US Council on Foreign Relations spearheaded a high-profile report sensationally entitled "Russia's Wrong Direction: What the United States Can and Should Do" (put out under the names of the politicians John Edwards and Jack Kemp). The document acknowledges that Washington's efforts to make Moscow into a (junior) partner for America's global agenda have failed. So the report recommends "selective co-operation" on issues for which Moscow could supposedly still be coaxed into doing the US bidding. At the same time, the report admits that the US faces a difficult task in the ancient mission of trying to rescue Russia from authoritarianism. And yet, despite how vital Russia seems to the US—in the report's illogic, precisely because of that very need—the democratisation of Russia must remain a US foreign policy goal. "To go beyond mere expressions about the rollback of Russian democracy," the report advises, "the US should increase—not cut—Freedom Support Act funds, focusing in particular on organisations committed to free and fair parliamentary and presidential elections in 2007–08."

Still more influential has been an essay published earlier this year [2008] in *Foreign Affairs*, "The Myth of the Authoritarian Model: How Putin's Crackdown Holds Russia Back" by Michael McFaul and Kathryn Stoner-Weiss. It is a rallying cry for America's besieged democracy-promoters, who are eager to regain the ground they lost after Iraq. The two authors are at pains to show that Putin's Russia is autocratic compared with Boris Yeltsin's "electoral" democracy (a telling modifier), and that Putin's autocracy has had nothing to do with Russia's economic success. This argument is a red herring. The point is not autocracy but the many vital economic liberalisation measures that were passed during Putin's first term (radical tax revision, red tape reduction, private property in land) as well as the maintenance of tough fiscal discipline and macro-economic stability. The authors downplay these breakthroughs (while also failing to note that second-term presidencies the world over are rarely known for continued bold policy achievements). McFaul, the lead author, seems unaware that his unsolicited concern for Russia continues more than a century of failed evangelism, as outlined by Foglesong. Indeed, McFaul and his co-author, both at Stanford, cannot be accused of excessive self-reflection: they condemn as "paranoid nationalism" Putin's straightforward observations regarding the "growing influx of cash used directly to meddle in our domestic affairs"—a policy that McFaul has taken part in and continues to advocate.

That McFaul and Stoner-Weiss must fight their democracy-promotion battle on economic grounds does not help their cause. When they assert that increased state ownership in the last few years has slowed Russia's economic performance, they underestimate the degree to which until very recently, Russian growth was helped by squeezing the last drops of blood from Soviet-era investments, a tactic that has stopped working. Moreover, excluding the two energy giants Rosneft and Gazprom, the increase in state ownership of companies in Russia is not dramatic. And many Russian state-owned firms, including the energy giants, are either at or set to reduce the state share in themselves to 51 per cent. (In 2007, Russian companies sold $33bn in stock flotations, mostly on international markets.) Russia's state-owned companies, too, whatever their dubious methods, have not been resting on their bureaucratic laurels but rather acquiring assets for the money (and ego). Of course, high debt accumulation to underwrite M&A [mergers and acquisitions] may not be a smart growth strategy (it sure looks stupid in the US). But as David Woodruff of the LSE [London School of Economics and Political Science] has pointed out, Russia's state-owned companies can redeem international capital market obligations only by increased market share and profits. They may turn out not to be up to the challenge. But hey, that's capitalism.

As their supposedly clinching argument, McFaul and Stoner-Weiss cite the circumstance that growth rates in Russia's neighbours have often been slightly better than Russia's—to wit, they write that from 1999 to 2006 Russia occupied ninth place among the 15 former Soviet republics in ranking of growth rates. The differences in growth and hence rankings are not that large, but let's accept them. The larger point, which the authors miss, is that these economies are all linked, so the authors need to take into account the impact of the large Russian economy's growth on these far smaller ones. In 2007, a half dozen or more of the former Soviet republics were utterly dependent on Russia as a source of remittances. More than 30 per cent of Tajikistan's GDP in 2007 consisted of remittances from Tajiks labouring in Russia. The estimate for remittances from Russia to Moldova was close to 30 per cent of GDP, for Kyrgyzstan more than 20 per cent, and for Georgia and Armenia probably between 10 and 20 per cent. And so on. Consider the possible effects if the millions of Ukrainians who have found work in Russia suddenly had to go home, unemployed. Comparable numbers for economic dependency are perhaps found only in the many countries receiving remittances from their nationals working in the US. There are many reasons to be critical of Russian economic performance and policies, but the super-high growth rate of Kazakhstan is not one of them.

Escaping the Past

In reality, though, McFaul and Stoner-Weiss are driven not by any interest in economics, but by the alleged urgency of democratisation for US foreign policy. In this regard, Robert Legvold, editor of the collection *Russian Foreign Policy in the Twenty-first Century and the Shadow of the Past*, published last year [2007], provides an echo. His introduction is a defence of a long overdue recourse to some history in analysing contemporary Russia. But even as he urges analysts to study Russia's past, he urges Russia "to escape its past," by which Legvold means its authoritarianism. Above all, he insists that the US and the EU [European Union] have "legitimate" interests in Russia's domestic political arrangements because of their impact on Russia's neighbours. (He might also have mentioned the impact on Russia's inhabitants, through international human rights policy.) In other words, Russian foreign policy, in Legvold's mind, flows not from the maw of Russian national interests but from the nature of its political system. Voilà. Here, projected outwards, we have hit upon one of those quintessentially American beliefs about itself: namely, that the US conducts itself in the world not on the basis of its national interests but on the basis of its democracy.

Not all the authors in the volume agree with Legvold that Russia's absolutism is unsuited to an era of globalisation. David McDonald portrays absolutism in Russia as a capacious toolbox, and one that today, too, can advance the country economically and culturally, even if such an approach carries the danger of overreach. Still, the general tenor of the volume falls in line with what Foglesong has shown to be an American-identity crusade projected on to Russia since 1881. Foglesong quotes David Lawrence, founder of *US News and World Report*, expressing the American establishment's underlying credo back in 1958: "There can be no safety in the world as long as we have autocratic regimes." This belief opens the widest possible field for a missionary foreign policy (and for the inevitable hypocrisy). It succeeded in uniting liberal internationalists, like McFaul and Stoner-Weiss, with neocons over Iraq, and like all fundamentalist beliefs, it survived that debacle. What it may not survive is the conversion of the American dollar into the Mexican peso.

The unsolved murders of Russian journalists and the arrests of political activists make many observers want at a minimum to chalk up Putin's boom to dumb luck—floating on highly priced reservoirs of oil and gas left by nature hundreds of millions of years ago—and to predict a comeuppance. Maybe Russia is set for a fall. In terms of quotidian state functions, Russia is badly governed, which makes it vulnerable in a crisis. In a global world where everything is connected, if China's boom loses air, Russia too will feel the enormous downdraught. And Wall Street's financial engineering may yet annihilate everyone, good and bad alike. Whatever the future holds, it is clear that the world has not seen such large authoritarian market economies like Russia's or China's since, well, Nazi Germany and its ally Japan. But today's authoritarian Russia and China are not militarily aggressive. And Edward Lucas notwithstanding, these countries are also not likely to be defeated in war and occupied so that the likes of Michael McFaul and Kathryn Stoner-Weiss can have another go at the democracy crusade so well chronicled by David Foglesong.

But Russia is not an EU country, not a US ally and not a China ally. It is perceived as a possible partner, but also as a potential enemy, by all three.

Russia's Economic Growth

The power of the Kremlin can seem all-encompassing. Across the 20th century, the average time in office for leaders in the democratic US has been about six years. In autocratic Russia, it has been around ten. Remove Stalin's long despotism, and the figure falls to eight. Still, authoritarian successions are always difficult from a regime's point of view. (Perhaps the most remarkable fact about China is not its market transformation but its two smooth, albeit opaque, political transitions after Deng Xiaoping stepped down, first to Jiang Zemin and then to Hu Jintao.) One of the many weak points of authoritarianism is that it makes bad options appear attractive—like hoping, as many do, that Putin remains Russia's real ruler. But whatever the fate of the latest succession, the Kremlin's China-like strategy will likely continue: suppressing many of the politically liberalising aspects of globalisation while pursuing its economic aspects to the ends of the earth.

Just like the Chinese and the Arab autocracies, the Russians are coming—and for real this time. When Russian capital, already highly visible in Europe and Britain, comes with ever greater force to Wall Street and to Main Street America, will Americans understand the value of Russia having a substantial stake in US success? Will Americans appreciate that having Russian-owned assets on American soil that could be seized provides a huge source of leverage over the Kremlin that is today lacking? As for the EU, it may be crucial for north Africa and the Levant [countries bordering the eastern Mediterranean], but it is far less so for Russia (or China). The EU seems likely to be bedevilled for some time over the status of Turkey, while Russia, just like China, continues to pursue bilateral relations with individual European countries. Russia's trade with EU countries is huge—three times its trade with the former Soviet republics—and Germany is easily Russia's biggest single partner (in 2007 their bilateral trade hit $52.8bn). Still, right now no place matters more to Russia than London as a commercial hub of globalisation. London's importance is one reason Russia has tried—with episodes like the British Council harassment—to send forceful diplomatic messages over anything related to its sovereignty, just as China does, without undermining real interests.

We should not, however, exaggerate Russia's global power. In future the US, the EU and China will each account for no less than one fifth of global GDP. Even if Russia does become the world's fifth largest economy, it would still constitute no more than 3 or so per cent of global GDP. The Kremlin will use its seat on the UN security council and presence at the G8 [a forum consisting of "Group of Eight" nations in the northern hemisphere] to defend its interests globally, while also seeking good relations with China in various forums. But Russia is not an EU country, not a US ally and not a China ally. It is perceived as a possible partner, but also as a potential enemy, by all three. Above all, if Russian companies, whether state-owned or private, are not able to go toe-to-toe with the best companies in the world, you can forget the whole game. "Even with the economic situation in our favour at the moment, we are still only making fragmentary attempts to modernise our economy," Putin said in a speech this year on Russia's long-term development strategy to 2020. "This inevitably increases our dependence on imported goods and technology, and reinforces our role as a commodities base for the world economy." He added that "the Russian economy's biggest problem today is that it is extremely ineffective. Labour productivity in Russia remains very low. We have the same labour costs as in the most developed countries, but the return is several times lower. This situation is all the more dangerous when global competition is increasing."

In short, President Medvedev and, if so named, Prime Minister Putin have their work cut out.

3

Russian Aggression May Spark a New Cold War

Mark Franchetti

Mark Franchetti is the Moscow correspondent of the Sunday Times *of London.*

While America was engaged in Iraq and Afghanistan, Russia refuted what it saw as Western meddling in its sphere of influence and invaded Georgia in August of 2008. The West has long tried to extend its influence in the countries of the former Warsaw Pact and tried to encircle Russia. Georgia's president, maybe hoping America would get involved, invaded South Ossetia, but when Russian troops attacked, America stood by helplessly, caught off guard. Russia's aggressive tactics threaten its neighbors and peace in the region, and America has neither the troops nor the strategy to counter them effectively.

Vadim, a South Ossetian militiaman, raced through the deserted Georgian streets, a Soviet Makarov pistol in one hand and a Kalashnikov [assault rifle] in the other. Dishevelled, unshaven and wild-eyed, he was searching for someone to kill. For the first time in 10 years he had crossed the border from his secessionist province and reached Gori, a town well inside Georgian territory, hours after it had been taken by Russian soldiers.

Wounded in the fighting, he had a gaping bullet hole in his upper thigh; but the pain only fuelled his thirst for revenge. As I sat by his side, he drove his battered Lada at high speed through Gori's bombed-out centre, often screeching to a halt to scour the side streets and buildings in search of defeated Georgian soldiers.

"This has been building up for years," he said. "I knew it would happen and I've been waiting for this moment for a long time. If I see a Georgian soldier I'll shoot his brains out. They're dogs."

As heavy artillery rounds exploded on the edge of town, we came across other civilian cars and minivans with Russian numberplates crammed with Vadim's fellow South Ossetian militiamen. Like Vadim, who was in a tattered camouflage uniform and white trainers, they looked wild and menacing. They wore white armbands to identify them to the Russian army as friendly forces.

Is the invasion of Georgia the first step towards an armed confrontation between America and Russia?

Horrifying Scenes

Some hid their faces behind black balaclavas [helmets]. It was the day after Dmitry Medvedev, Russia's president, had called an end to military operations in Georgia. American humanitarian aid was flowing in. Yet the Russians still occupied about a third of Georgia with impunity and Vadim and his cohorts were on the rampage in horrifying scenes that evoked the Balkan wars of the 1990s.

Not only had America and its NATO [North Atlantic Treaty Organization] partners been shamed by the invasion of a country that had been welcomed into the Western embrace, but they had also shown themselves incapable of sending home the Russians and their henchmen. This humiliation raises far-reaching questions about American power, Russian revanchism and Europe's sometimes craven relationship with the Kremlin.

However, the most important question is one that Washington seems unable to answer: what is its long-term purpose in relations with Russia? Does America want Moscow as a global partner, particularly in the war on terror and in repressing Iran's nuclear ambitions? Or is it pursuing a strategy of containing the Russian bear by close alliances with neighbouring countries that were once Kremlin satrapies [tax districts]?

"Realist" diplomats from Henry Kissinger downwards are pointing out that America can't do both because a contained Russia won't be a cooperative Russia. However, if Georgia were to join NATO, the consequence could be a much more serious confrontation with Moscow, as the alliance works on the understanding that an attack on one member is an attack on all. Is the invasion of Georgia the first step towards an armed confrontation between America and Russia?

On Friday [August 15, 2008], Russia even threatened Poland with nuclear retaliation for agreeing to host US rockets as part of its antimissile shield. Not that Vadim cared about the geo-political picture. He shouted obscenities at a frightened young woman as we drove by in a side street.

The Timeline of the Crisis

"Wouldn't mind f***ing one of these Georgian girls," he said. When the history of the conflict comes to be written, it may be that a small incident on the road linking Georgia to Tskhinvali, the capital of South Ossetia, will be identified as the starting point of war. The US State Department's internal timeline of the crisis pinpoints the explosion on August 1 [2008] of two roadside bombs, believed to have been planted by South Ossetian separatists sympathetic to Russia, as a decisive moment. Five Georgian policemen were injured, one severely.

That night Georgian forces struck back. There was a furious firefight that left six South Ossetian rebels dead. Condoleezza Rice, the [former] secretary of state, was on holiday. A few new provocations by the South Ossetians did not appear to warrant her coming home. The US intelligence services had been warning that the Russians were preparing for war, but it did not occur to them that fighting would break out just as the world was settling down to watch the Beijing Olympics.

Moscow argues that while it pulled back its troops from eastern Europe and allowed American forces into central Asia to fight in Afghanistan, the Americans have been invading [Russia's] traditional sphere of influence.

It now appears that August 1 was a well-prepared "provocation"—one of the Kremlin's favourite tactics. Pavel Felgengauer, a Moscow authority on military affairs, claimed in *Novaya Gazeta* that the plan was for the "Ossetians to intentionally provoke the Georgians" so that "any response, harsh or soft, would be used as an occasion for the attack." At last Russia was going to teach the Georgians a lesson. Moscow's relations with the tiny nation of 5m[illion] had begun to deteriorate when Mikheil Saakashvili swept to power [as president of Georgia] nearly five years ago.

A US-educated lawyer aged 40 [in August 2008], Saakashvili is fervently pro-Western. Washington has encouraged his aspirations to join NATO and has helped to train the Georgian army with the help of the Israelis. [Former] President George W. Bush visited Georgia, promising to stand by it, and relations between Saakashvili, the State Department and the Pentagon have been close. Vladimir Putin has watched the process with mounting anger.

Russia's Sphere of Influence

Moscow argues that while it pulled back its troops from eastern Europe and allowed American forces into central Asia to fight in Afghanistan, the Americans have been invading [Russia's] traditional sphere of influence.

"It's a very emotional issue," said a Western diplomat. "Most Russians, not just the Kremlin, see Georgia as part of their world and take the fact that most Georgians aspire to join NATO as an act of betrayal. Add the paranoia about the West wanting a weak Russia and conspiring to encircle it and you have an explosive situation. On the other hand, Georgians clearly aspire to closer relations with the West because they fear Russia."

Saakashvili has long vowed to bring South Ossetia and Abkhazia, another pro-Russian separatist region flanking the Black Sea, back under [the Georgian capital] Tbilisi's control. His populist pledge is supported by most Georgians. "Georgia is nothing without Abkhazia [a de facto independent state within Georgia's internationally recognized border] and South Ossetia," said Levan, a Georgian trapped in Gori when the Russians moved in last week.

"Imagine someone came and ripped your arm off. That's what it's like for us. These two regions are an integral part of Georgia and must be returned to us."

The stakes were raised this year when Kosovo gained independence, prompting Putin to increase support for Georgia's breakaway republics. That came as an increasingly bullish Saakashvili prepared an assault to retake parts of Abkhazia. Western diplomatic sources last week [in August 2008] revealed that in early May [2008], Washington had put frantic pressure on the Georgian leader to stop him [from] launching military operations.

"They only just managed to stop him," said a source.

By the summer, attention had switched to South Ossetia. Russians and Georgians accused each other of straying into each other's territory. Rice told Saakashvili at a private dinner on July 9 [2008] not to respond with military force. However, while she thought that her message was loud and clear, Saakashvili went on to thank her warmly for her "unwavering support for Georgia's territorial integrity" and may have interpreted it as permission to act as he pleased. Within three weeks the clashes of August 1 had raised tension again.

"The American position should have not just been clear, but imperative."

Growing Tensions

Rice remained on holiday while Daniel Fried, the assistant secretary of state, took the role of keeping Georgia calm. Saakashvili also spoke on the phone to President Nicolas Sarkozy of France, which [at the time held] the European Union presidency, and to Javier Solana, the EU foreign policy chief.

Western sources say neither they nor the Americans could restrain him; but the Georgian leader last week angrily said he had repeatedly warned Washington and EU countries that the Russians were preparing a military operation against Georgia but that he had been brushed aside.

On August 7 [2008] Fried took a call from Eka Tkeshelash-vili, the 31-year-old Georgian foreign minister, who told him Russian tanks were advancing on South Ossetia in what appeared to be preparations for an attack. Fried warned her to avoid war but the message did not sink in, sources say. Ariel Cohen, a Russian expert at the conservative Heritage Foundation in Washington, said there should have been direct talks with Saakashvili.

"They needed to be at a very high level, not at the level of Mr. Fried. The American position should have not just been clear, but imperative." A few hours after the call to Fried, in the early hours of Friday August 8, Georgia launched its offensive in South Ossetia, killing many civilians; and Russia responded with a huge show of force, bombing Georgia and invading a sovereign country for the first time since it seized Afghanistan in 1979.

Tskhinvali lay in ruins last week, bearing evidence of both the Georgian attack and the Russian counterattack. The remains of Georgian armoured vehicles lay upside down close to the central square. Witnesses told of cars filled with fleeing Ossetian refugees being shelled by Georgian tanks.

War Atrocities

They claimed that in one incident Georgian soldiers finished off the wounded by pouring fuel over them and burning them. Independent human rights observers confirmed that civilian targets had been repeatedly hit, including basements where terrified residents had sought refuge and were trapped for days. Moscow has claimed that some 2,000 people died at the hands of Georgian forces—including 15 Russian peacekeepers.

However, Human Rights Watch, the American group, said that Russian estimates were "suspicious."

America had sleepwalked into a foreign policy disaster and its response was slow and uncertain. With [George W.] Bush tarrying in Beijing watching the Olympics while Putin executed a war, Americans were reminded uncomfortably of Hurricane Katrina—another occasion when [George W.] Bush dithered before eventually getting around to sending humanitarian aid.

Ralph Peters, a former military intelligence analyst, said last week [August 2008] at a symposium on Georgia at the neoconservative American Enterprise Institute: "The image for me will be the president going to a basketball game and flirting with the beach volleyball team."

He added: "Vladimir Putin is the most effective leader in the world today. Nobody comes close. In contrast, President [George W.] Bush is looking like [former U.S. president] Jimmy Carter when the Soviets invaded Afghanistan. It's tragic."

False Assumptions

[George W.] Bush had thought he had Georgia in his pocket. Saakashvili is surrounded by US civilian and military advisers and is so close to US politicians that John McCain, the Republican [2008 presidential] nominee, claimed last week [August 2008] to be in daily telephone contact with him. However, he is regarded as "mercurial"—a polite way of saying that the Americans lost control of their client. "We'd been warned about Saakashvili for some time. Our advisers knew he wasn't ready for prime time," said Peters. "But he's the democratically elected leader of Georgia.

"The Russians knew they could poke him and poke him until he responded." It was the Europeans who moved first in trying to stop the fighting. At the Olympic opening ceremony on August 8 [2008], Sarkozy bumped into Putin soon after news of Georgia's offensive in South Ossetia started coming in. "Sarko" was with 11-year-old Louis, his youngest son, and the Russian prime minister wrapped the boy in a bear hug.

Nearby, [George W.] Bush was looking through binoculars at the Olympic parade. "Listen," Sarkozy told Putin, "it's a mistake by Saakashvili. We have to find a way out of this crisis."

An implacable Putin replied: "I can't let it happen." After returning from China to France, Sarkozy called Angela Merkel of Germany, Silvio Berlusconi, the Italian prime minister, Spain's Jose Luis Rodriguez Zapatero and 10 Downing Street [London office and residence of the United Kingdom's prime minister] to try to work out a European reaction to the fighting. In reality, the crisis had split Europe along the fault line that has divided it since the Iraq war. Germany, with its close commercial ties to Russia, wanted a "no blame" solution.

A Divided Front

Poland empathised with Georgia, and Britain stood by Washington in firmly condemning the invasion. France not only has a policy of engagement with Russia but was also enjoying taking the diplomatic front seat. Sarkozy got back on the phone to Medvedev in Moscow.

The Russian president wanted Saakashvili "fired," but Sarkozy told him that was not a helpful condition. "It's not up to you or me to designate the Georgian leader," he told the Russian. Washington apparently tried to persuade Sarkozy not to go to Moscow to talk to Russia's leaders face to face.

"For the first time in a major international crisis, it is the Americans who are on the touchline [sidelined] and it is the European Union that is being called upon to sort things out."

[George W.] Bush warned him: "You'll arrive at the Kremlin when the Russians are firing missiles at Tbilisi." Sarkozy went anyway and was apparently told by Putin at a working lunch in the Kremlin on Tuesday: "It's just like in the films—there's a good cop and a bad cop," referring to himself and Medvedev.

Even so, the "nice" Medvedev did not mince his words. In a press conference later that day he referred to Saakashvili as a madman. "The difference between madmen and normal people," he explained, "is that madmen, when they smell blood, it is very difficult to stop them."

Despite the rhetoric, Russia accepted an EU-sponsored accord. "For the first time in a major international crisis, it is the Americans who are on the touchline [sidelined] and it is the European Union that is being called upon to sort things out," crowed a French presidential aide. Well, perhaps: the Russians might have agreed to a deal but they had not yet delivered on it.

Continued Fighting

Gori is a town of more than 50,000 people, 40 miles north of Tbilisi. When I entered it on foot last Wednesday [August 13, 2008], five days after the Russians' invasion, their troops were advancing rather than withdrawing.

A few hours earlier a column of Russian armoured personnel carriers, mounted with large calibre machineguns and carrying hundreds of troops, had crossed the border despite assurances from Moscow that it would not stray into Georgia proper. They took Gori without fighting, as Georgian troops fled in [the] thousands.

Plumes of black smoke rose on the edge of town as Russians took up position on a ridge, setting fire to the surrounding fields. As I walked by the roadside towards the city, armoured vehicles packed with soot-covered Russian soldiers cradling AK47s and grenade launchers rumbled past, their tracks crushing the asphalt. One came to a halt and its commander offered me a lift. I jumped on the back and rode a couple of miles towards the town centre.

"The Georgians asked for it," Sergei, a soldier from Siberia, yelled over the engine. "They came into Tskhinvali, destroyed it and killed a hell of a lot of civilians. What did they expect—for Russia to sit back? As far as I'm concerned we should go all the way to Tbilisi and take the city. We should wipe them out and teach them not to mess with Russia."

Famed as Stalin's birthplace, Gori was a bustling community before hostilities broke out. Last week it was a ghost town. I passed blackened apartment blocks that had been hit by Russian bombs. Laundry was still hanging out to dry, abandoned in the panic. I came across fewer than 100 people.

"We haven't eaten in three days; do you have any bread? Please help," said an elderly woman dressed in black who was too scared to try to leave the town. A small group of men huddled in a yard, looking shellshocked and incredulous at the sight of Russian tanks taking up positions a few hundred yards down the road. Koba, a 35-year-old worker, said they had spent much of the past two days hiding in their cellar for fear of Russian bombing. . . .

In South Ossetia itself, vengeful militiamen were moving into deserted ethnic Georgian villages on what they said was a mopping-up operation to "find Georgian saboteurs and looters."

As they advanced they carried out widespread looting and burnt houses in an apparent ethnic cleansing campaign to ensure locals did not return. A group of militiamen held a Georgian soldier prisoner in the back of a truck, his mouth covered with a filthy T-shirt to block out the stench of two rotting corpses lying beside him—fellow Georgian soldiers clad in NATO camouflage uniforms.

"I didn't kill anyone. I didn't kill your women and children. I swear," he said, pleading with his captors to spare him. Inal, a militia sergeant, was in no mood for concessions. "You're going to be dumping your comrades' bodies soon, you faggot, where we only bury stray dogs. And that's where you are soon going to join them."

Burying the Dead

The prisoner was made to drag the dead men off the truck and to bury them in a ditch with the corpses of eight other Georgian soldiers. Some were stripped naked and charred. One had his mouth still open in a grimace of terror and pain. "Tell us the f***ing truth. Where is your weapon? Where are your documents? If you don't tell us the truth, we'll shoot you dead," Inal, 47, yelled at the prisoner, who claimed to have been responsible only for food and transport. Inal was unconvinced. "We'll talk to you properly back at the base. Then we'll see if you are telling the truth."

The road to the military base deep inside Russian-controlled South Ossetia was scattered with rotting Georgian corpses. Inal paraded two more prisoners—both middle-aged men. One, with a scar across his nose and broken lips, was shaking in fear as Inal began the interrogation. He sat both men on the ground and took off the safety catch on his Kalashnikov.

America now has to decide how to contend with the newly resurgent Russia.

The two Georgians, who were not wearing military uniforms, said they were builders from a nearby hamlet who had been caught in the fighting and had lost their IDs. Yelling, Inal hit one hard in the face. The man groaned in pain and cowered behind his friend's shoulders.

"Where is your weapon, you faggot?" Inal barked, threatening to drown the man in a pool. But another South Ossetian soldier stopped Inal and handed the prisoner a NATO ration pack. "Made in the USA! Enjoy!" he laughed. At first the Russian army appeared unable or unwilling to control the militias. On Thursday [August 14, 2008], after the Russian interior minister said looters should be dealt with severely, soldiers blocked the road from South Ossetia into Georgia to paramilitary forces and arrested several looters.

America now has to decide how to contend with the newly resurgent Russia and with a self-confident Vladimir Putin. Whether he is called president or prime minister is immaterial. He is "Tsar Vladimir" or, as *The Wall Street Journal* put it, "Vladimir Bonaparte." Robert Gates, the US defence secretary, ruled out the use of force last week to compel Russia to return to the status quo ante.

Georgia's Future Is in Doubt

For now the two breakaway provinces are back in Russia's orbit, and a question mark hangs over the future of Georgia and other former Soviet satellite states. Some American commentators believe that their country's performance has been shameful. Nile Gardiner, director of the Margaret Thatcher Centre for Freedom at the Heritage Foundation, said: "The Iron Lady [Thatcher] would never have stomached this sort of behaviour by the Russians. She would have issued an immediate statement condemning Moscow, summoned an urgent meeting of the NATO command and demanded that the Russians halt their advance and withdraw their forces or face the consequences."

The [George W.] Bush administration ... preferred to utter general warnings about Russia's imperilled standing in the world rather than to deliver specific threats to curb its behaviour.

According to Gardiner, "The whole episode has demonstrated to eastern Europe that America and NATO won't protect it. It sends the message that it is open season on any of the border states and that the West doesn't have the stomach to protect them."

The rapid conclusion of long negotiations between America and Poland to site American missile defences on Polish territory last week showed the gravity of the crisis for countries that used to be behind the Iron Curtain. "Poland and the Poles do not want to be in alliances in which assistance comes at some point later. It is no good when assistance comes to dead people," said Donald Tusk, the Polish prime minister.

The historian Leon Aron, an expert on Russia, said: "The next target of opportunity is Ukraine—not the entire country, but the Crimean peninsula and Sebastopol, which is home to the Black Sea fleet." There is talk about suspending Russia's membership of the G8 or boycotting the 2014 Winter Olympics, which will be in Sochi, in southern Russia; but the [George W.] Bush administration ... preferred to utter general warnings about Russia's imperilled standing in the world rather than to deliver specific threats to curb its behaviour.

"Will NATO and the EU draw the conclusion that we should stay away from the former Soviet states in order not to be drawn into a conflict, or will they decide that they ought to offer them the protection of membership? I'm not optimistic," said Aron. [George W.] Bush [had] barely five months of his presidency left—not enough time for a tired administration, still grappling with Iraq, Iran and the intractable Palestinian problem, to come up with a coherent policy on the resurrection of Greater Russia. It seems certain that Vadim and his ragtag cohorts will be celebrating the events of August 2008 for years to come.

4

The New Cold War Might Be a Russian Stunt

Paul du Quenoy

Paul du Quenoy is a professor in the Department of History and Archaeology at the American University of Beirut.

While its recent actions have created international tensions, Russia does not have the economic or military power and stamina to enter a new cold war. Oil and gas revenues have not stabilized the market, and much of its weapons arsenal is old and in disrepair. The invasion of Georgia does not disguise that Russia is not the superpower it once was.

Dmitrii Medvedev, the Russian president, says he is not afraid of a new cold war.

Should anyone be?

The recent [August 2008] conflict in Georgia and the surging rhetorical battle between Moscow and Western leaderships have revived ugly twentieth-century memories.

But it is perhaps worth recalling German unification chancellor Otto von Bismarck's warning that Russia is never as strong or as weak as it looks. As we approach the spectre of a new cold war, however, we can rest confident that Russia's strength is of the exaggerated quality.

Last week, Russian bombers landed in Venezuela. After mauling its former colony of Georgia, Russia is now reaching out to a Latin American well-wisher, whose leader spoke positively of its actions and just severed diplomatic relations with Washington.

Paul du Quenoy, "Who's Afraid of a New Cold War," *Al Jazeera English*, September 18, 2008. Reproduced by permission of the author.

Ugly shadows of the Cuban Missile Crisis, we are told, loom over the tranquil Caribbean.

As we approach the spectre of a new cold war . . . we can rest confident that Russia's strength is of the exaggerated quality.

One would have to read far into most news stories, however, to learn that Russia's "power projection" consists of just two Tu-160 bombers, which were entered into service in 1987.

Almost as old as the classic film *Top Gun*, their stated purpose is to train over neutral waters for a few days and then return to Russia.

Hugo Chavez, the Venezuelan president and a former air force general himself, plans to fly "one of those monsters," as he calls them, and excitedly announced that "Yankee hegemony is finished."

Pale Reflection

Obviously, this is no Cuban Missile Crisis. In 1962 Nikita Khrushchev, the Soviet leader, secretly sent nuclear missiles to communist Cuba. American U-2 spy planes discovered the deployment.

In a tense moment, the US blockaded Cuba to prevent more missiles from arriving and presented solid evidence of the existing missiles to the United Nations.

Within a few days the Soviets backed down and withdrew their weapons in exchange for a US promise to remove outmoded missiles from Turkey.

Two years later Khrushchev's colleagues removed him from power, blaming him for having both brought their country to the brink of nuclear war and backed down in what they called "a humiliation."

Last week's flight to Venezuela is a pale reflection of that cold war flashpoint.

It falls more safely into the "stunt" category—potentially dramatic, but lacking both substance and lasting effect. In a few days the twin Tu-160s will be back in Russia.

Given Russia's current military potential, stunts of this type and invading small neighbours will likely remain the limit of its activity.

Seventy per cent of Russian military personnel are still terribly underpaid conscripts. Forcibly enlisted new soldiers are subjected to violent hazing (a harassing initiation ritual), which kills hundreds of them every year (292 in 2006) and seriously injures thousands more.

Faltering Russian Hardware

Soviet-era equipment will not be phased out of use until 2020. Most of Russia's navy has rotted in port since the collapse of the Soviet Union.

Only 26 of Russia's 50 remaining submarines (compare to 170 in 1991) are currently operational, and the Russian navy plans to reduce that number to 20.

Like the Tu-160s in Venezuela, Russia's combat aircraft are for the most part decades old.

Only 15 of Russia's latest and most sophisticated fighter jets, the Sukhoi-35s, are in active service. Russia's tank arsenal is still dominated by the antiquated T-72, which entered production in 1971 and was the backbone of Iraq's ill-fated army in 1991 and 2003.

Despite significant increases, Russia's defence budget is less than one-tenth the amount of annual US military spending.

According to a Russian Defense Ministry spokesman, the Tu-160s that just flew across the Atlantic were even "escorted" by NATO fighter jets.

NATO Supporting Georgia

Closer to home, Medvedev and Vladimir Putin, the prime minister, face the reality of US and NATO support pouring into Georgia even as their own forces complete their withdrawal from Georgian territory.

Their warnings to Western powers to steer clear of the crisis have been dismissed. The Caucasus pipeline continues to pump oil outside the Russian state monopoly that once controlled all former Soviet energy exports to the West.

Mikhail Saakashvili, the Georgian president, who is pro-Western and George Washington University-educated, remains firmly in power, more than a month after Russia's foreign minister bluntly said "he has to go."

Medvedev and Putin will soon have to live with deployments of anti-missile defence systems in Poland and the Czech Republic—deployments accelerated by the Georgia crisis.

They know that a majority of Ukrainians now favour NATO membership, whereas only a few weeks ago the issue was divisive in that country. They can be reasonably certain that their evolving peaceful relationship with NATO and the civilian nuclear-sharing agreement with the US are now, effectively, dead.

Financial Upheaval

[Also dead] is their long-coveted inclusion in the World Trade Organisation, from which they have withdrawn their membership bid rather than face the humiliation of having it vetoed.

They must wonder about the nature of their relationships with China and the ex-Soviet Central Asian republics, which, despite Medvedev's begging at an emergency meeting of [the] Shanghai Cooperation Organisation last month [August 2008] refused to support Russian policy and instead backed the French-sponsored ceasefire.

Finally, Russia's leaders will have to deal with the $500 billion drop in market values following their attack on Georgia, most of which represents hastily withdrawn foreign investments and domestic capital flight abroad.

These figures were current before the catastrophic economic news of earlier this week, when high energy price-dependent Russian markets fell even further and registered their worst losses since the financial crisis of 1998.

In Venezuela, Chavez will soon be back to worrying about his precarious domestic position. Less than a year ago he lost his own referendum.

Trading had to be suspended on Monday and Wednesday [September 2008], and the biggest losers were government-controlled energy companies, Russia's only serious hard currency earners.

The Kremlin may secretly wonder whether more than half a trillion dollars is the right price to pay to be able to call the shots in Tskhinvali (pre-conflict population: 30,000), but so far its major move has been for Medvedev to announce increased military spending while trying to reassure a roomful of nervous oligarchs who know better that there is no financial crisis.

A History Repeat?

In Venezuela, Chavez will soon be back to worrying about his precarious domestic position. Less than a year ago he lost his own referendum, which would have amended Venezuela's constitution to eliminate term limits on his presidency and vastly expand his government's economic powers to control banking and expropriate private property.

He plans to leave office in 2013, in accordance with the pre-referendum requirement. Like Putin, he may try to replace himself with a hand-picked successor who, like Medvedev, will have to campaign for election.

Karl Marx famously wrote that "history repeats itself, first as tragedy, second as farce."

The last cold war was tragic for much of the globe. If there is another one, it will almost certainly be a farce for Russia, which, in addition to the problems outlined above, has tried to replace its lost ideology with a grasping obsession with the "order" and "security" that its ex-KGB functionaries imagine to have been benefits of their Soviet experience.

Whether or not a new cold war comes, Medvedev already has a lot to fear within his borders.

Just across the border, Condoleezza Rice, the [former] US secretary of state, and Radek Sikorski, the Polish foreign minister, recently celebrated the signing of a bilateral missile defense agreement by drinking Georgian wine over dinner.

5

The U.S. Missile Defense Program May Trigger a New Cold War

George Monbiot

George Monbiot is the author of Heat: How to Stop the Planet Burning, The Age of Consent: A Manifesto for a New World Order, *and* Captive State: The Corporate Takeover of Britain. *He writes a weekly column for the* Guardian *newspaper.*

The U.S. missile defense system, to be installed in Poland officially to shoot down North Korean or Iranian missiles, is a poorly disguised threat to Russia. Unfortunately, the British government, after the recent disasters in Afghanistan and Iraq, will again lend support to misguided American adventures. The missile defense system will do nothing to stabilize global safety, but it might bring about another cold war.

In one short statement to parliament last week, the defence secretary, Des Browne, broke the promises of two prime ministers, potentially misled the House, helped bury an international treaty and dragged Britain into a new cold war. Pretty good going for three stodgy paragraphs.

You probably missed it, but it's not your fault. In the 48 hours before parliament broke up for the summer, the government made 76 policy announcements.(1) It's a long-standing British tradition: as the MPs and lobby correspondents are packing their bags for their long summer break (they don't return until October), the government rattles out a series of important decisions which cannot be debated. Gordon Brown's promise to respect parliamentary democracy didn't last very long.

Far from making the world a safer place, its [US missile defense] purpose is to make the annihilation of another country a safer proposition.

Thus, without consultation or discussion, the defence secretary announced that Menwith Hill,* the listening station in Yorkshire, will be used by the United States for its missile defence system.(2) Having been dragged by the Bush administration into two incipient military defeats, the British government has now embraced another of its global delusions.

Des Browne's note asserted that the purpose of the missile defence system is "to address the emerging threat from rogue states." This is a claim that only an idiot or a member of the British government could believe. If, as Browne and Bush maintain, the system is meant to shoot down intercontinental missiles fired by Iran and North Korea (missiles, incidentally, that they do not and might never possess), why are its major components being installed in Poland and the Czech Republic? To bait the Russian bear for fun? In June, Vladimir Putin called Bush's bluff by offering sites for the missile defence programme in Azerbaijan and southern Russia, which are much closer to Iran.(3) Bush turned him down and re-stated his decision to build the facilities in eastern Europe, making it clear that their real purpose is to shoot down Russian missiles.

Nor is it strictly true to call this a defence system. Russia has around 5,700 active nuclear warheads.(4) The silos in Poland will contain just 10 interceptor missiles. The most likely strategic purpose of the missile defence programme is to mop up any Russian or Chinese missiles which had not been destroyed during a pre-emptive US attack. Far from making the world a safer place, its purpose is to make the annihilation of another country a safer proposition.

This strategic purpose takes second place to a more immediate interest. Because it doesn't yet work, missile defence is the world's biggest pork barrel. The potential for spending is unlimited. First a number of massive—and possibly insuperable—technical problems must be overcome. Then it must constantly evolve to respond to the counter-measures Russia and China will deploy: multiple warheads, dummy missiles, radar shields, chaff, balloons and God knows what. For the US arms industry, technical failure means permanent commercial success.

Like the war with Iraq, the US missile defence programme exacerbates the threats it claims to confront.

But this is not the only respect in which Browne appears to have misled the House. He claimed to have assurances from the US that "the UK [United Kingdom] and other European allies will be covered by the system elements they [the Americans] propose to deploy to Poland and the Czech Republic." Browne must be aware that this is a United States missile defence programme. It incorporates no plans for defending other nations. The British government has handed over its facilities, truncated parliamentary democracy and put its people at risk solely for the benefit of a foreign power.

The diplomatic cost of this idiocy is incalculable. It has already required the abandonment by the US of the Anti-Ballistic Missile Treaty, which is the bilateral agreement struck between the United States and the Soviet Union in 1972. It survived both the vicissitudes of the Cold War and the collapse of the Soviet Union, but not George W. Bush. Any hope that it might be revived has now been buried by the facts on the ground in Poland, the Czech Republic and the United

Kingdom. Two weeks ago Vladimir Putin suspended another long-standing agreement: the Conventional Armed Forces in Europe Treaty, which limited the troops and military hardware Russia could assemble on its borders. In response to the US missile defence programme, Russia has also been testing a new version of its short-range Iskander nuclear missile, and it has been developing a new intercontinental missile with multiple warheads, called the RS-24. Their purpose, according to Sergei Ivanov, the deputy prime minister, is to "overcom[e] any existing or future missile defence systems" (5). The Iskander missiles will be deployed on the European border and aimed at Poland and the Czech Republic. Intermediate-range missiles will be pointed at Menwith Hill.

Bush's missile defence programme almost certainly means the end of the intermediate-range nuclear forces treaty as well, and the cancellation of any successor to the strategic offensive reductions treaty (which expires in 2012). Asked whether this might be the beginning of a new cold war, Putin replied, "Of course we are returning to those times. It is clear that if a part of the US nuclear capability turns up in Europe, and, in the opinion of our military specialists will threaten us, then we are forced to take corresponding steps in response. . . . We are not the ones who are initating the arms race in Europe."(6) Like the war with Iraq, the US missile defence programme exacerbates the threats it claims to confront.

All this, as you would hope, is of some interest to our members of parliament, who have long been demanding a debate. In February, Tony Blair agreed that they would have one. "I am sure that we will have the discussion in the House and, indeed, outside the House. . . . When we have a proposition to put, we will come back and put it."(7) In April, Des Browne told MPs that "the UK has received no request from the US to use RAF Menwith Hill for missile defence-related activities."(8) That, until last week, was all that parliament knew. Now we discover that the proposition had been made and accepted before MPs had a chance to discuss it. Browne was in the House on Wednesday, where he made some announcements about aircraft carriers and the military budget. These—because they were delivered in person—could be discussed, though (shamefully) neither of them provoked any opposition.(9) But knowing that the Menwith Hill decision would be furiously opposed, Browne released it in the form of a written statement, which cannot be debated.

Like everyone on the left in Britain, I wanted to believe that Gordon Brown's politics would be more progressive than Tony Blair's. But as he grovels before the seat of empire, I realise that those of us who demand even a vaguely sane foreign policy will find ourselves in permanent opposition. With his appointment of Digby Jones as trade minister and his plans for deregulation, Brown demonstrated that the government is still mesmerised by big business. By proposing that suspects be held for up to 56 days without charge, he appears to share Tony Blair's distrust of liberty. Now, in one furtive decision, he reveals both his contempt for parliament and his enthusiasm for the neocon project. What, I wonder, is there left to hope for?

*Correction (Published August 2nd 2007) attached to this article: The Menwith Hill intelligence-gathering station is not on the the North York Moors, as we said in a Comment piece, Brown's contempt for democracy has dragged Britain into a new cold war, page 25, July 31. It is west of Harrogate.

6

Russia Will Lose If It Enters a New Cold War

Matthew Lynn

Matthew Lynn is a Bloomberg News *columnist. The opinions expressed are his own.*

Russia's military response to the invasion of South Ossetia by Georgian troops was disproportionate, and can only be regarded as an attempt to reestablish itself as a power to be reckoned with. But the new nationalism, which will isolate Russia further, will harm its own population the most. Its already weakened economy might not withstand a renewed cold war.

Aug. 13 (Bloomberg) After sending tanks, troops and warplanes into Georgia last week, Russian President Dmitry Medvedev yesterday ordered a halt to the ground offensive.

By the standards of military conflicts in the region, it was a short one. The Caucasian War of the 19th century, when Russia expanded its influence in the region, lasted from 1817 to 1864.

Yet just because this one was short—and it remains to be seen whether the cease-fire holds—doesn't mean its impact won't be long-lasting.

Russia is threatening a new Cold War by dispatching troops to the independent state of Georgia. The trouble is, there isn't much reason to think it will do better this time around than it did in its Cold War with the U.S. and the West last century. We will all be poorer if there is more tension between Russia and the rest of the world. And Russia will suffer most of all.

The main facts of the conflict are clear enough. Russia sent its soldiers into the breakaway Georgian region of South Ossetia after Georgian soldiers started an offensive. According to Medvedev, Georgia was starting "genocide" there. Russian troops went in to protect ethnic Russians.

There may have been some legitimacy to the original Russian case. Yet trying to portray its army as a kind of revved-up Swiss peace-keeping force won't strike many people as very convincing. Nor does Prime Minister Vladimir Putin make a plausible champion of the rights of oppressed minorities. If he worries so much about the suffering of innocent people, it is strange we never saw that side of the former president's personality before.

We will all be poorer if there is more tension between Russia and the rest of the world. And Russia will suffer most of all.

A Disproportionate Response

It is hard to see Russia's response as anything other than disproportionate. It looks like a crude attempt to re-establish control over a country that was part of the 19th-century Russian empire, and part of the Soviet Union as well, but which in the last decade had allied itself with the U.S. and European Union.

Former Soviet leader Mikhail Gorbachev let the cat out of the bag with an article in the *Washington Post* newspaper this week when he argued that Russia had "legitimate interests in this region" and that the U.S. had committed a "serious blunder" by treating the Caucasus as being within its sphere of national influence.

And yet, all the talk of concepts such as "legitimate interests" and "spheres of interest" just shows how stuck in the past Russia is. This is steam-age, great-power diplomacy, not information age, peaceful co-operation.

Putin's Nationalism

Britain used to think it had "legitimate interests" in Ireland. Nazi Germany used to suppose it had "legitimate interests" in Poland (and quite a few other places, come to think of it). Fortunately, Western Europe has moved on from that nonsense. Neighboring countries have shared interests in promoting the free movement of people and goods to increase prosperity for everyone. They don't have "legitimate interests" that allow them to send tanks across borders.

This is yet another example of Putin's aggressive style of Russian nationalism. We have seen it with gas supplies to Ukraine, and with the hounding of oil companies such as Royal Dutch Shell Plc and BP Plc over their investments in Russia. Now we are seeing it in Georgia as well.

Russia may be aggrieved that Georgia is part of the U.S.-backed "southern energy corridor" that connects the Caspian Sea region with world markets, bypassing Russia. It wants to use oil as a way of re-asserting its great-power status. That, surely, is a mistake of historical proportions.

Putin and his cronies may believe they are making Russia strong again. Instead, they are turning it into a pariah state.

Oil to Build

It should be using its oil wealth to rebuild its infrastructure and education system, creating a modern economy, one that can still prosper after we have all switched to running our cars on nuclear-powered and wind-generated electricity. It doesn't matter to Russia whether Georgia shares in the region's oil wealth any more than it mattered to Britain that the Norwegians also controlled a lot of the oil in the North Sea. What matters is using the oil money to build your own economy.

This may mark the high tide of Putin nationalism. The Russian stock market soared on the news of the cease-fire in Georgia. The ruble started to recover. Yet both the currency and the stock markets have still been hammered over the past few weeks. Investors are taking flight at the authoritarian behavior of the regime. The treatment of companies such as BP—whose joint venture TNK-BP was the subject of various disputes in Russia—will deter foreign investors from the country.

Putin and his cronies may believe they are making Russia strong again. Instead, they are turning it into a pariah state. Yet if there is one thing we know for certain, it is that the path to prosperity is through peace and trade, not through military posturing. Pariah states are also poor states.

Russia lost the last Cold War and will lose this one as well, if tensions continue. It doesn't have the money or the manpower, and without guns, steel and bodies, all wars, whether cold or hot, are eventually lost. Russia will postpone its integration into the developed world by a generation or more— and both sides will be the poorer for that.

7

Russian Aggression Represents a New Era but Not a New Cold War

Robert Marquand

Robert Marquand is a staff writer for the Christian Science Monitor.

Despite recent crises, caused by military aggression and weapons programs, the Cold War is a thing of the past. The relationship between Russia and America has evolved since the Cold War, and Russia needs the Western economies for its economic gain. While Russia wants its place in the global arena, it doesn't want to antagonize possible partners and allies.

Two weeks into the Georgia crisis [August 22, 2008], Russia maintains leverage, adroitly playing a great game of obfuscation and tit-for-tat—both militarily and diplomatically—with a disunited West struggling to determine whether this is a new cold war.

Vladimir Putin's idea of the 21st century appears different from that described by President [George W.] Bush in calling for Russia to withdraw. As NATO officials this week fought to show strong support for Georgia without irreparably damaging ties to Russia, the "new world order" described by Mr. Bush's father as the Soviet empire collapsed seems a faint memory.

Robert Marquand, "Why Georgia Is Not the Start of 'Cold War II,'" *Christian Science Monitor*, August 22, 2008 Copyright © 2008 The Christian Science Publishing Society. All rights reserved. Reproduced by permission from *Christian Science Monitor*, (www.csmonitor.com).

Yet while Russia's action has been termed a new cold war, that concept doesn't capture the dramatic global changes since Mikhail Gorbachev disbanded the Soviet Union in 1991, say diplomats and Russian area specialists. In a more globalized world, Russia is at once a competitor, a partner, and an opponent.

"It is the greatest challenge for any statesman today to see what is the right priority," says Pierre Hassner, a Paris-based scholar of East-West relations. "Is it Iran, Russia, the price of oil, terrorism? It may in some ways look like the cold war again—but the context today is blurred past recognition."

This week [in August 2008], rhetoric and emotion escalated: As Poland and the US signed a missile shield deal Tuesday [August 18, 2008], Moscow said Russia "will be forced to react, and not only through diplomatic means"—and is hosting Syria's president today to discuss further military cooperation.

NATO chief Jaap de Hoop Scheffer said this week it will no longer be "business as usual" with Moscow, and German Chancellor Angela Merkel in Tbilisi defied Russia threats over NATO expansion and said Georgia will "one day" be a member. Russian Foreign Minister Sergei Lavrov shot back that "NATO is trying to make a victim of an aggressor [Georgia] and whitewash a criminal regime."

World dynamics in the cold war versus those in 2008 are as different as the transistor radio and the iPod.

Muddled View of Moscow's Intent

Meanwhile, Moscow's intent in Georgia remains unclear. Russian troops on the ground have contradicted official promises; Russian authorities have avidly reinterpreted a French-brokered cease-fire. It remains unclear whether troops will withdraw into South Ossetia, or create their own unbrokered security zone in a swath of Georgia outside Ossetia. Moscow first said its troops would pull out, then said troops would only pull back. All the while, Russian forces have moved freely on Georgian territory and taken control of several cities. The delay is widely seen as a bid to dramatize the West's inability to deter. Georgian President Mikheil Saakashvili called the delay an opportunity for Moscow to "laugh at" the West.

Russian military authority remains split between a president elected in [March 2008] with no opposition and Prime Minister Putin, who once called the breakup of the Soviet Union "the greatest catastrophe of the 20th century."

Such remarks may feed new definitions of a "cold war," as does Putin's putative intent to exert power and influence in weaker states around Russia—particularly any Eurasian oil corridors through Georgia that would deny lucrative tariffs for Moscow.

Radio vs. IPod

Yet world dynamics in the cold war versus those in 2008 are as different as the transistor radio and the iPod. The interlinked economies of Russia and Europe, vastly freer global media access, the rise of China, greater travel, new generations, disparate wealth, and changed attitudes and expectations—make a different world than during the rigid standoff between the liberal West and communist Soviets. Russia is no longer a self-contained empire animated by the discipline of socialist morality—far from it, and the West is no longer focused on a single opponent. Issues without borders, such as energy, the environment, terror, trade, banking, and mafias—emerged more strongly after the Berlin Wall went down. The West needs Russia's help to constrain Iran.

The term cold war itself may actually block new thinking, argues Paul Goble, a former State Department and CIA analyst and expert on Soviet nationalities.

"The Russian Federation and the United States are not about to enter a new cold war even if tensions between Moscow and Washington rise dramatically," says Mr. Goble. "The cold war pitted an ideologically driven Soviet Union against the free world, a conflict [where] both sides . . . devoted enormous resources to defeat the other."

"References to the cold war now are . . . unhelpful . . . ," [and] he adds, "an ideologically driven notion that the only possible choices these two countries have for relations are total conflict or total agreement, neither of which is possible or desirable."

In Poland, [former] Secretary of State Condoleezza Rice told reporters, "I don't think this is a new cold war."

In France, President Nicolas Sarkozy warned of the risk of a "new cold war" days ago, but has not repeated the phrase. French foreign affairs analyst Daniel Vernet, writing in *Le Monde*, argues that Russia is acting more like "a czarist power" than a Soviet power—and says the phrase "cold war" is useful to Moscow, since it conceptually divides [eastern and western] Europe into old zones of influence in which each side can act with relative impunity.

In the post-cold-war world of 2008, there's no one overarching reality that provides an orienting stability.

"We are stuck in relationships in which major powers are not enemies, but not friends," says Mr. Hassner at the Center of International Studies and Research in Paris. "The UN isn't working. The new world order and the democracy surplus never came to be—but there are networks of capital and cooperation between Russia, China, and the West that weren't there before."

A New World

To be sure, thinkers—diplomats, scholars, writers—say the Russian blitz into Georgia represents a new world, but what kind of new world is undefined.

Cold war certainties have given way to an international climate that is mixed up, unpredictable, contrary, and quite corrupt. Russia's action is creating "a new context of fear rippling through its border regions," says Goble, causing "effects we can't even understand yet."

In the post-cold-war world of 2008, there's no one overarching reality that provides an orienting stability. Russians again feel Moscow's power and authority, and are assured by it. Wars in Iraq and Afghanistan make NATO, the US, and Europe appear weak. In this world, "if you take one action, it can boomerang and harm something else," says Hassner. The "war on terror" isn't an adequate principle around which to center all focus, he adds.

Some East European analysts say Russia doesn't want to attack or allow hostile relations with the West à la cold war; rather, Moscow's intent is to exploit the riches and technology of the West.

"Russia's strength is made possible by oil at $150 a barrel," says Bartosz Weglarczyk, foreign editor of influential Polish daily *Gazeta Wyborcza*. "If oil is cut to $60 a barrel, Russia is sunk. [Russians] spend less on research and development than Poland. They want bank accounts in the West, to make [millions] off sales to Europe. They don't want a big war. They want to gain influence and manipulate."

8

Russia Is Too Weak to Enter Another Cold War

Jack Snyder

Jack Snyder is the Robert and Renee Belfer Professor of International Relations at Columbia University.

The question whether there will be a new cold war or not depends on American diplomacy. Only if the U.S. misinterprets Moscow's posturing as a serious threat to global security will a new cold war arise. Russia's economy is too weak and dependent on the West to allow its leaders another arms race with America. While the U.S. should help democratic states of the former Soviet Union enter NATO, it should not try to blindly win over allies in Russia's sphere of influence, further antagonizing its leaders. Europe should seek alternative fuel sources in order to free itself from Russian oil and gas supplies.

Will there be a new cold war with Russia? Only if the United States responds to Russia's limited coercive behavior with an aggressive strategy of rigid containment. Russia is too weak to mount a serious geopolitical challenge to the United States or to the Europeans, and it lacks the motivation to do so.

Russia is a weak, two-dimensional power, drawing on its superficial oil wealth and on the remnants of the Soviet military industrial complex. It is hobbled by Russia's profound demographic crisis, which Vladimir Putin is doing nothing to correct. It is limited by the fact that Russian financial power is totally dependent on income from oil and gas exports to its potential geo-political rivals, Europe and possibly, in the future, China. It is hampered strategically by the mixed blessing of autocracy, which on one hand permits Russia to concentrate its resources on whatever foreign policy task the autocrat decides to prioritize at the moment, but on the other hand hamstrings social and economic innovations that are needed to turn Russian into really a first-rank player in the world.

Joseph Stalin made a famous and prescient speech in 1931, noting that Russia had always been beaten for its backwardness, and that it would have ten years to make up centuries of relative backwardness before it would be attacked again. Stalin's speech revealed the two sides of backwardness for Russia: On one hand, we're beaten because we're backward technologically and economically. On the other hand, we have the advantage of backwardness, because I'm a strong autocrat, and I can whip the society to make it take a leap of centuries in only ten years.

The Disadvantages of Backwardness

But nowadays, Russia has only the disadvantages of backwardness with none of the advantages, because Putin is not whipping Russian society to force it to innovate, to get the Russian people to contribute to some enterprise of national power. Putin is just happy to have the Russian people lie placidly and stay out of his way as he collects oil revenues. This is not an adequate strategy if you want to embark on a cold war with America.

Russia lacks any attractive social purpose to mobilize mass support for a foreign policy in Russia itself, let alone to serve as a model for other societies to emulate or to provide any ideological reason to ally with Russia. This is not the Soviet Union, which did have a purported social purpose that seemed attractive to some. And Russia today is not a country that has mass nationalism to induce people to contribute and sacrifice for any strategic goal.

In this situation, Russian foreign policy will probably be characterized by a desire to maintain stable long-term relations with its energy customers abroad. Russia will undertake efforts to enhance its position of regional quasi-monopoly over gas supplies, especially for the Europeans.

The prescription that follows from this analysis is that the West should try to develop alternative energy sources for Europe so that Putin cannot step on that toe whenever he wants.

The Russians may engage in coercive political, economic, and even military tactics of a limited sort to serve that purpose. Russian policy will include attempts to undermine democratic government in neighboring states that implicitly threaten Russian political legitimacy. Mainly, this means Georgia and Ukraine; it does not mean Estonia as long as Estonia's Russians stick with their current strategy of gradual integration into Estonian society and as long as the ethnic Estonians are nice to the Russians who live in their country. [What it] also will likely mean [is] Russian attempts to create a sphere of influence in its near abroad [neighbor nations] to limit encroachments by NATO. And it will probably mean, from time to time, the revival of Russia's shallow alliances with anti-Western states, maybe in the Middle East, maybe elsewhere, which are useful for commercial reasons and for diplomatic leverage.

Nikita Khrushchev used to say that it was a great advantage for Russia that West Berlin existed, because it was an exposed toe that Russia could step on whenever it needed to annoy the West and extract concessions. And Putin's Russia will probably look for opportunities to play that strategy, not in Berlin, but somewhere else, perhaps Iran or elsewhere.

The Dangers of Post-Putin Russia

My main worry is that when the Putin system collapses, which eventually it will because it is a house of cards built on a wasting oil resource, there will be a jockeying of Russian political rivals to create some new form of legitimate rule that is very unlikely to resemble liberal democracy.

There is no evidence of a constituency for liberal democracy in Russia. Even in the 1990s, when they had a political system that contained some of the features of democracy, public attitude surveys showed that the Russians did not highly value free speech and democracy itself; they just wanted to have a stable regime that would increase their standard of living. When the Putin system unravels, new elites may want to warm their hands on the fires of nationalism, because that could be a trump card in jockeying for power. The Russian people are not nationalist by nature.

They're very inert. They are hard to whip up in that way. [Russian nationalist politician] Vladimir Zhirinovsky tried and did not get very far with it. Nonetheless, Russian nationalism after Putin is what I worry about the most.

The prescription that follows from this analysis is that the West should try to develop alternative energy sources for Europe so that Putin cannot step on that toe whenever he wants.

The West should stop the rhetoric of both friendship and enmity with Russia, and replace it with language of limited rivalry that can be managed by pragmatic bargaining. We should state the West's willingness to cooperate fully with any regional states—meaning Russia, Ukraine, Georgia, and whoever—that consolidate true liberal democracy and meet strict standards of European Union and NATO membership with respect to rule of law, non-corruption, minority rights, and free speech. But we should not gild the lily in describing countries like Ukraine and Georgia as if they were already fully democratic or likely candidates for full democratic consolidation really soon. And we should not take on the task of reforming these states as if they were already our allies or our protectorates. In particular, we should not engage in rhetorical or actual confrontations with Russia that would tend to lock in an attitude of enmity with the broad mass of the Russian people, possibly stoking a nationalist revival in the post-Putin future.

9

The Cold War Will Be Staged in the Arctic

Ariel Cohen, Lajos Szaszdi, and Jim Dolbow

Ariel Cohen is a senior research fellow in Russian and Eurasian Studies and International Energy Security. Lajos Szaszdi is a researcher in the Douglas and Sarah Allison Center for Foreign Policy Studies at The Heritage Foundation. Jim Dolbow is a defense analyst and a member of the Editorial Board at the U.S. Naval Institute.

The Arctic holds vast oil and gas resources, and America should expand its presence there to secure its energy interests. Russia, with a mixture of aggression and international law, has laid claims to much of the Arctic. Its renewed military aggression might pose a challenge to American claims in the Arctic. Russia has resumed a warship presence and ignores NATO members' sphere of influence there. Therefore, it would be of great importance to form an alliance with Canada to secure energy resources and police the region. America needs to affirm its position in the Arctic and take on a leadership role in Arctic energy exploration.

The Arctic is quickly reemerging as a strategic area where vital U.S. interests are at stake. The geopolitical and geoeconomic importance of the Arctic region is rising rapidly, and its mineral wealth will likely transform the region into a booming economic frontier in the 21st century. The coasts and continental shelf of the Arctic Ocean are estimated to

Ariel Cohen, Lajos Szaszdi, and Jim Dolbow, "The New Cold War: Reviving the U.S. Presence in the Arctic," *Heritage Foundation, Backgrounder #2202*, October 30, 2008. Copyright © 2008 The Heritage Foundation. Reproduced by permission.

hold large deposits of oil, natural gas, and methane hydrate (natural gas) clusters along with large quantities of valuable minerals.

With the shrinking of the polar ice cap, extended navigation through the Northwest Passage along the northern coast of North America may soon become possible with the help of icebreakers. Similarly, Russia is seeking to make the Northern Sea Route along the northern coast of Eurasia navigable for considerably longer periods of the year. Opening these shorter routes will significantly cut the time and costs of shipping.

In recent years, Russia has been particularly active in the Arctic, aggressively advancing its interests and claims by using international law and by projecting military might into the region.

Despite the Arctic's strategic location and vast resources, the U.S. has largely ignored this region. The United States needs to develop a comprehensive policy for the Arctic, including diplomatic, naval, military, and economic policy components. This should include swiftly mapping U.S. territorial claims to determine their extent and to defend against claims by other countries. With oil and gas prices recently at historic highs in a tight supply and demand environment, the rich hydrocarbon resources in the Arctic may bring some relief to consumers. These resources, especially the hydrocarbons, also have the potential to significantly enhance the economy and the energy security of North America and the world.

The Arctic's Vast Untapped Resources

The U.S. Geological Survey estimates that the Arctic might hold as much as 90 billion barrels (13 percent) of the world's undiscovered oil reserves and 47.3 trillion cubic meters (tcm) (30 percent) of the world's undiscovered natural gas. At current consumption rates and assuming a 50 percent utilization rate of reserves, this is enough oil to meet global demand for

1.4 years and U.S. demand for six years. Arctic natural gas reserves may equal Russia's proven reserves, the world's largest.

In recent years, Russia has been particularly active in the Arctic, aggressively advancing its interests and claims by using international law and by projecting military might into the region.

The Russian Ministry of Natural Resources estimates that the underwater Arctic region claimed by Russia could hold as much as 586 billion barrels of unproven oil reserves. The ministry estimates that proven oil deposits "in the Russian area of water proper" in the Barents, Pechora, Kara, East Siberian, Chukchi, and Laptev Seas could reach 418 million tons (3 billion barrels) and proven gas reserves could reach 7.7 tcm. Unexplored reserves could total 9.24 billion tons (67.7 billion barrels) of oil and 88.3 tcm of natural gas. Overall, Russia estimates that these areas have up to 10 trillion tons of hydrocarbon deposits, the equivalent of 73 trillion barrels of oil.

In addition to oil and gas, the Arctic seabed may contain significant deposits of valuable metals and precious stones, such as gold, silver, copper, iron, lead, manganese, nickel, platinum, tin, zinc, and diamonds. The rise of China, India, and other developing countries has increased global demand for these commodities.

Alaska's North Slope

Alaska's North Slope contributes significantly to U.S. oil production and could supply more. The North Slope is the region of Alaska from the Canadian border on the east to the Chukchi Sea Outer Continental Shelf (OCS) on the west. It includes the Chukchi Sea OCS, the Beaufort Sea OCS, the Arctic National Wildlife Refuge (ANWR), the Central Arctic (the region between the Colville and Canning Rivers), and the National Petroleum Reserve, Alaska.

Between 1977 and 2004, the Prudhoe Bay oil field on the North Slope produced more than 15 billion barrels of oil. By 1988, Prudhoe Bay was accounting for more than 25 percent of U.S. crude oil production. However, Prudhoe Bay oil field is currently in steep decline. A U.S. Department of Energy report found that the North Slope has potentially 36 billion barrels of oil and 3.8 tcm of natural gas, close to Nigeria's proven reserves. The report also estimates that the Chukchi Sea OCS and the Beaufort Sea OCS hold combined energy reserves of 14 billion barrels of oil and about 2 tcm of natural gas.

To enhance U.S. energy security, America should expand domestic oil production.

Furthermore, these reserves are even more attractive because their development is less limited by federal, state, and local legislation, as is the case with ANWR, and are thus more accessible to drilling.

To enhance U.S. energy security, America should expand domestic oil production. America remains the only oil-producing nation on earth that has placed a significant amount of its reserves out of reach. Until recently, potentially large U.S. natural gas deposits have been off limits. For instance, ANWR holds potential reserves of about 10 billion barrels of petroleum. Such reserves could lead to an additional 1 million barrels per day in domestic production, which could be transported south through the Trans-Alaska Pipeline, which has a spare capacity of 1 million barrels per day. An additional 1 million barrels per day would save the U.S. $123 billion in petroleum imports, create $7.7 billion in new economic activity, and generate 128,000 new jobs. . . .

U.S. Claims in the Arctic

The U.S. relies on its sovereign power and diplomacy when pursuing territorial claims in the Arctic. The United States is not a party to the United Nations Convention on the Law of the Sea Treaty (LOST) and therefore is not bound by any procedures and determinations concluded through LOST instruments. Instead, the U.S. is pursuing its claims "as an independent, sovereign nation," relying in part on Harry S. Truman's Presidential Proclamation No. 2667, which declares that any hydrocarbon or other resources discovered beneath the U.S. continental shelf are the property of the United States. The U.S. can defend its rights and claims through bilateral negotiations and in the multilateral venues such as through the Arctic Ocean Conference in May 2008, which met in Ilulissat, Greenland.

Many have argued, including the [George W.] Bush Administration, that the U.S. will not have leverage or a "seat at the table" to pursue or defend its Arctic claims on condition that the U.S. is not a party to LOST. However, U.S. attendance at the conference in Ilulissat significantly weakened this argument. Even though the U.S. is not a LOST party, other Arctic nations "are unable to assert credible claims on U.S. territory in the Arctic or anywhere else in the world" because President Truman already secured U.S. rights to Arctic resources with his proclamation.

The U.S. relies on its sovereign power and diplomacy when pursuing territorial claims in the Arctic.

Yet to protect its rights, the U.S. needs to know how far its claims stretch into the Arctic Ocean. The U.S. has been mapping the bottom of the Arctic Ocean and the Outer Continental Shelf since 2003. Mapping is essential to determining the extent of the U.S. OCS and determining whether the U.S. has any legitimate claims to territory beyond its 200-nautical-mile exclusive economic zone. Despite ongoing U.S. efforts to chart the bottom of the Arctic Ocean, mapping efforts have been inadequate. According to a National Research Council report in 2007, the U.S. continental shelf and the Northwest Passage have not yet been entirely mapped. Mapping is also important for disputing any conflicting claims by other Arctic nations. For example, the U.S. and Canada have likely claimed some of the same parts of the continental shelf. Mapping data will also help to determine whether Russian claims conflict with U.S. and Canadian claims.

The expedition undertaken by the icebreaker USCGC *Healy* in the Chukchi Sea focused on surveying an area 400 to 600 miles north of Alaska and cost about $1.2 million—a pittance compared to the billions of dollars of Arctic natural resources that are at stake. The survey indicated that the foot or lowest part of the Alaskan continental shelf stretches more than 100 miles beyond what was previously thought, thus expanding the U.S. claim.

The U.S. requires a modern flotilla of icebreakers to conduct mapping and to sustain U.S. claims. The U.S. currently has only three icebreakers that belong to the Coast Guard, of which only the *Healy* (commissioned in 2000) is relatively new. The other two icebreakers, while heavier than the *Healy* and thus capable of breaking through thicker ice, are at the end of their designed service life after operating for about 30 years. Yet even if the U.S. begins now, it will be eight to 10 years before a new icebreaker can enter service, and no money has been allocated to build a new-generation heavy icebreaker.

Russian Claims

After its invasion of Georgia, Russia has clearly hardened its international posture and is increasingly relying on power, not international law, to settle its claims. Moscow has also intensified its anti-American policies and rhetoric and is likely to challenge U.S. interests whenever and wherever it can, including in the High North.

Russia takes its role as an Arctic power seriously. In 2001, Russia submitted to the U.N. Convention on the Law of the

Sea a formal claim for an area of 1.2 million square kilometers (460,000 square miles) that runs from the undersea Lomonosov Ridge and Mendeleev Ridge to the North Pole. This is roughly the combined area of Germany, France, and Italy. The U.N. commission did not accept the claim and requested "additional data and information." Russia responded by sending a scientific mission of a nuclear-powered icebreaker and two mini-submarines to the area. During this meticulously organized media event, the mission planted the Russian flag on the ocean's floor at the Lomonosov Ridge after collecting soil samples that supposedly prove that the ridge is part of the Eurasian landmass. During the mission, Deputy Chairman of the Russian Duma Artur Chilingarov, the veteran Soviet explorer heading the scientific expedition, declared, "The Arctic is ours and we should demonstrate our presence." Such statements run counter to the spirit and potential of international cooperation and seem inappropriate for a scientific mission.

The U.S. has objected to these claims and stated that they have "major flaws." Professor Timo Koivurova of the University of Lapland in Finland stated that "oceanic ridges cannot be claimed as part of the state's continental shelf." Russia intends to resubmit its claim by 2009.

After its invasion of Georgia, Russia has clearly hardened its international posture and is increasingly relying on power, not international law, to settle its claims.

Russia is also moving rapidly to establish a physical sea, ground, and air presence in the Arctic. In August 2008, Russian President Dmitry Medvedev signed a law that allows "the government to allocate strategic oil and gas deposits on the continental shelf without auctions." The law restricts participation to companies with five years' experience in a region's continental shelf and in which the government holds at least a 50 percent share, effectively allowing only state-controlled

Gazprom and Rosneft to participate. President Medvedev also featured the Arctic prominently in the new Russian Foreign Policy Concept, which states: "In accordance with the international law, Russia intends to establish the boundaries of its continental shelf, thus expanding opportunities for exploration and exploitation of its mineral resources."

During 2008, Russian icebreakers . . . constantly patrolled in the Arctic. Russia has 18 operational icebreakers, the largest flotilla of icebreakers in the world. Seven are nuclear, including the *50 Years of Victory*, the largest icebreaker in the world. Russia is planning to build new nuclear-powered icebreakers starting in 2015. Experts estimate that Russia will need to build six to 10 nuclear icebreakers over the next 20 years to maintain and expand its current level of operations. Russia's presence in the Arctic will allow the Kremlin to take de facto [actual] possession of the underwater territories . . . in dispute.

In addition to icebreakers, Russia is constructing an Arctic oil rig in the northern shipbuilding center of Severodvinsk, which will be completed by 2010. The rig will be the first of its kind, capable of operating in temperatures as low as minus 50 degrees Celsius (minus 58 degrees Fahrenheit) and withstand the impact of ice packs. The new rig was commissioned by the state-controlled Gazprom and demonstrates that Russia is serious about oil exploration in the Arctic.

Russia's Polar Saber Rattling

In August 2007, shortly after sending the scientific expedition to the Arctic ridge, [Russia's then] President Vladimir Putin ordered the resumption of regular air patrols over the Arctic Ocean. Strategic bombers including the turboprop Tu-95 (Bear), supersonic Tu-160 (Blackjack), and Tu-22M3 (Backfire) and the long-range anti-submarine warfare patrol aircraft Tu-142 have flown patrols since then. According to the Russian Air Force, the Tu-95 bombers refueled in-flight to extend their operational patrol area. Patrolling Russian bombers penetrated the 12-mile air defense identification zone surrounding Alaska 18 times during 2007. Since August 2007, the Russian Air Force has flown more than 90 missions over the Arctic, Atlantic, and Pacific Oceans.

Warship Presence in the Arctic

The Russian Navy is also expanding its presence in the Arctic for the first time since the end of the Cold War. Lieutenant General Vladimir Shamanov, head of the Defense Ministry's combat training department, said that the Russian Navy is increasing the operational radius of the Northern Fleet's submarines and that Russia's military strategy might be reoriented to meet threats to the country's interests in the Arctic, particularly with regard to its continental shelf. Shamanov said that "we have a number of highly-professional military units in the Leningrad, Siberian and Far Eastern military districts, which are specifically trained for combat in Arctic regions."

On July 14, 2008, the Russian Navy announced that its fleet has "resumed a warship presence in the Arctic." These Arctic naval patrols include the area of the Spitsbergen archipelago that belongs to Norway, a NATO member. Russia refuses to recognize Norway's right to a 200-nautical-mile exclusive economic zone around Spitsbergen. Russia deployed an anti-submarine warfare destroyer followed by a guided-missile cruiser armed with 16 long-range anti-ship cruise missiles designed to destroy aircraft carriers.

The resumption of Cold War–style patrols and increased naval presence in the Arctic is in keeping with Moscow's more forward posture and is intended to increase its leverage vis-à-vis [in relation to] territorial claims. Moscow is taking a dual approach of projecting military power while invoking international law. Regarding the naval deployments near Spitsbergen, the Russian Navy stated:

Sorties of warships of the Northern Fleet will be made periodically with a necessary regularity. All actions of the Russian warships are fulfilled strictly in accordance with the international maritime law, including the UN Convention on the Law of the Sea.

At a meeting of the Russian government's Maritime Board in April 2008, Russian Foreign Minister Sergei Lavrov backed a policy of settling territorial disputes in the region with the countries bordering the Arctic through cooperation. First Deputy Prime Minister Sergei Ivanov, who is now deputy prime minister, stressed at the meeting that Russia observes the international law on the matter through adherence to "two international conventions": the 1958 Convention on the Continental Shelf, signed by Canada, Denmark, Norway, Russia, and the U.S., and the 1982 U.N. Convention on the Law of the Sea.

While paying lip service to international law, Russia's ambitious actions hearken back to 19th-century statecraft rather than the 21st-century law-based policy and appear to indicate that the Kremlin believes that credible displays of power will settle the conflicting territorial claims. By comparison, the West's posture toward the Arctic has been irresolute and inadequate.

Moscow is taking a dual approach of projecting military power while invoking international law.

Arctic Sea-Lanes

The Arctic Ocean has two main sea routes that are open to shipping for about five months of the year with the help of icebreakers: the Northern Sea Route and the Northwest Passage.

The Northern Sea Route links the Barents Sea in the west with the Chukchi Sea to the east and services isolated settlements along Russia's long Arctic coastline. If the Arctic ice cap continues to shrink, it will become a major route for international shipping. A Northern Sea Route that is navigable longer would make the transportation of commodities to international markets easier and significantly reduce transportation costs between the Pacific Rim and Northern Europe (and Eurasia).

A Russian Information Agency Novosti political commentator argued:

> The country that dominates this sea lane will dictate its terms to the developers of the shelf deposits and will see the biggest gains from the transportation of raw materials to the Pacific and the Atlantic. These include billions of tons of oil and trillions of cubic meters of gas, not to mention other minerals in which the local lands abound.

Another Russian expert similarly lamented, "If we do not start immediately reviving the Arctic transportation system, voyages on the Northern Sea Route will be led by the Japanese or the Americans."

The Northwest Passage runs through Canada's Arctic archipelago. If the polar ice cap continues to recede, the Northwest Passage will become a major shipping lane for international trade between Europe and Asia, cutting transit times substantially. Currently, navigation is possible along the Northwest Passage during a seven-week period with the use of icebreakers.

According to a report by the U.S. Office of Naval Research, by 2050 "[t]he Northwest Passage through the Canadian Archipelago and along the coast of Alaska will be ice-free and navigable every summer by non-icebreaking ships."

Use of the Northwest Passage is a contentious issue between the United States and Canada. The U.S. argues that "it is a strait for international navigation" because it regards the Northwest Passage as international waters. Canada, on the other hand, claims that the straits of the sea route are "inland seas" falling under Canadian sovereignty. Resolving this dispute amicably is essential for both countries to benefit from further economic and security cooperation.

International Cooperation

The United States has a strong interest in cooperating with its Arctic neighbors, especially Canada, in developing offshore oil and gas fields and policing the region. Canada is a close NATO ally and a reliable oil and natural gas supplier to the United States. Canada also maintains a very friendly investment climate compared to other energy-producing nations. Opening the Arctic is a major opportunity for U.S. and Canadian companies to enhance the energy security of North America.

At a recent conference, Robert McLeod, former minister of energy of Canada's Northwest Territories, said that exploitation of the oil and gas resources in the Arctic would improve North American energy security and that "[t]he combined northern gas reserves in Canada and the United States could supply southern markets in Canada and the United States with 8 billion cubic feet per day."

Opportunities also exist for cooperation in defense and national security. As during the Cold War, the U.S. could work with its NATO partners in the Arctic region. This is already taking place at the U.S. Air Force base in Thule, Greenland, under bilateral agreements between the U.S. and Denmark that facilitate this cooperation. The U.S. and Canadian Coast Guards resupply the Thule Air Base. The most important example of U.S.-Canadian defense cooperation is the North American Aerospace Defense Command (NORAD). The Alaskan NORAD Region is regaining its former relevance with the Russian bomber incursions.

Warmer ocean temperatures and a smaller ice cap would also provide increased opportunities for U.S.-Canadian maritime cooperation in combating potential terrorist operations and unlawful navigation. Moreover, warming of the northern portion of the Bering Sea may induce the migration of fish to the Arctic Ocean, opening opportunities for joint fishing regulation. With the North Pacific already suffering from extensive poaching, unlawful fishing could become a problem. Joint law enforcement coordination for commercial fishing will be increasingly important. . . .

Opening the Arctic is a major opportunity for U.S. and Canadian companies to enhance the energy security of North America.

Reestablishing the U.S. Arctic Presence

As an Arctic nation, the United States has significant geopolitical and geo-economic interests in the High North. The U.S. should not only have a place at the table, but also seek a leadership role in navigating the nascent challenges and opportunities, such as disputes over the Outer Continental Shelf, the navigation of Arctic sea-lanes, and commercial development of natural resources and fisheries.

To play this role and to vindicate its interests, the U.S. needs to continue swiftly mapping the Arctic, build a modern U.S. icebreaker fleet, and work with its Arctic partners in bilateral and multilateral venues. The U.S. needs to revitalize its Arctic policy and commit the necessary resources to sustain America's leadership role in the High North.

10

The New Cold War Will Be Waged over Control of Energy Resources

Paolo Pontoniere

Paolo Pontoniere is a New America Media European commentator.

The new cold war is fought over energy resources, and already Russia has gained enormous leverage with Europe, which is dependent on its oil and gas. As a major oil producer, Russia is also trying to gain influence in countries of the former Soviet Bloc, and it is trying to expand its control of the Arctic. Yet Russia isn't trying to return to the old Cold War, and the West should not provoke any major altercations, since Russian influence could severely compromise U.S. access to oil reserves of newly independent countries such as Georgia and Kazakhstan.

A new Cold War is under way, but unlike the conflict of the [President Ronald] Reagan era it is not a fight for military supremacy but rather for gaining control, directly or through commercial proxy, of energy resources.

At the heart of this new conflict are Western attempts to diffuse Russian President Vladimir Putin's drive to transform his country into a new oil and gas superpower with vast bargaining power with the European Community. Russia is already the world's eighth largest producer of crude oil and the [largest producer] of natural gas.

Most recently, UK [United Kingdom] authorities blamed Russian intelligence for the assassination of Alexander Litvinenko, a former KGB spy, who had accused Vladimir Putin of leading an autocratic, murderous and corrupt government. Litvinenko was a figure in the struggle between the Putin government and Russian oligarchs (whom Western powers favor) for the country's most prized possessions—the oil and gas fields controlled by the Russian oil companies, the state-controlled Gazprom and the privately held Yukos.

Litvinenko's assassination nearly coincided with the signing of a commercial agreement between Gazprom and ENI—Italy's largest energy conglomerate—for the distribution of natural gas to Western Europe. The first of its kind, the agreement would allow Gazprom to operate independently under the supervision of the Italian partner, which would be tantamount to the Russian giant selling its product directly to consumers in Western Europe, bypassing EU's [European Union's] regulatory constraints.

Militarization of the Arctic

Western powers have come to despise what they see as Russia's heavy-handed form of capitalism, as in the case of mining rights to the Arctic sea floor, which is believed to hold vast oil reserves. According to Moscow, under the newly operating United Nations Convention on the Law of the Sea, more than 50 percent of those submerged resources belong to Russia. This assertion has compelled other powers—such as Denmark, Norway, Canada and Iceland—to stake their own claims to some of the same underwater territories. The controversy is leading to an increased militarization of the Arctic, with Russian battleships often confronting the vessels of oil developers and Western navies.

"Putin has decided to make a huge energy superpower out of Russia and there's almost nothing that can stop him," says Robert Hueber, an analyst at the Centre for Security and International Studies. "Unless something slows him down, there's no way for the West to prevent him from putting his hands on some of the most prized resources of the planet."

Although China's higher profile in Africa is providing cause for concern to the United States and its allies, it is Russia that generates their strongest reactions. They believe Russia is using its energy clout for geopolitical gains, especially in the regions that were once under the Soviet control but are now independent countries.

Western powers have been vehemently denouncing Russia for last year's rows with Ukraine and Belarus over the price of gas. Russia temporarily shut down its gas and oil shipments to these countries as a result of the quarrel. The action in turn caused great worry and anger in Western Europe, which imports respectively 30 percent of its oil and 40 percent of its gas from Russia.

In some countries like Poland, Finland and Slovakia, imports account for more than 70 percent of consumption, and in Hungary the percentage soars above 89 percent. Reacting to the shutdown, Germany's Chancellor Angela Merkel said Russia had lost its credibility as an energy partner.

Although China's higher profile in Africa is providing cause for concern to the United States and its allies, it is Russia that generates their strongest reactions.

Western analysts have also accused Moscow of conspiring to turn the Shanghai Cooperation Organization—an intergovernmental body composed of China, Russia, Kazakhstan, Kyrgyzstan and Tajikistan, with India, Pakistan and Iran as invited observers, meant to foster good neighborly relations and deal with issues of Central Asian security—into a sort of "OPEC with nuclear weapons," as described by Simon Sweeney, director of the International Studies Programme of York St. John University College in the United Kingdom.

Not all analysts, however, are convinced that Russia wants to wage a new Cold War with the West and in particular with the United States.

Russia Is Not Interested in a Cold War

"Someone is still fighting the Cold War, but it isn't Russia," Mark Almond, a professor of modern history at Oriel College, Oxford, wrote in *The Guardian*. "The chill is still coming from the West."

Thomas Friedman, a devout pro-West observer, agrees. Should Moscow, he writes, really decide to leverage its energy resources to subjugate the international community, it would have other, sharper arrows in its quiver.

Russia could, as many of its hardliners have suggested, ban products from Moldova and Georgia or block the transit of their unemployed jobseekers to Russia, thus causing these countries' economic collapse. Moscow could also destabilize Georgia, Ukraine, Moldova and Kazakhstan and then agree to annex—as these populations have requested—their pro-Russian minorities living near the borders of the old Motherland.

In the case of Georgia and Kazakhstan, destabilization could be extremely hard on the United States and its Western allies, as it would totally compromise direct access to the immense oil resources of the Caspian region—on which the West is greatly reliant—and their transfer to Western ports.

Thus, for now, and short of an all-out confrontation with the Old Bear, the Western powers can only lash out at the feared expansionism of the New Oil Czar by accusing Moscow of renewed charges of murderous plots and dark conspiracies.

11

A Cold War Could Prove Dangerous for Azerbaijan

Kaveh Afrasiabi

Kaveh Afrasiabi is the author of After Khomeini: New Directions in Iran's Foreign Policy.

Amid worries about a new cold war waged between Russia, America, and Europe, Azerbaijan finds itself in a precarious situation. While Europe clamors to build the Nabucco Gas Pipeline, connecting the Caspian Sea's gas resources with European users, to gain independence from Russian and Iranian resources, Russia and Iran oppose such a project, claiming that their own pipelines are sufficient, and that new pipelines would carry great ecological risks. Azerbaijan would gain from a new pipeline, as it is trying to build stronger ties to the West, but it can't risk offending Russia and a possible political isolation, or, worse, a military intervention. Diplomacy will be key to Azerbaijan's future.

Azerbaijan's presidential elections are a few weeks away [October 15, 2008], and while most experts agree it is a sure bet that the current president, Ilham Aliyev, will easily win re-election [Aliyev claimed an overwhelming percentage of votes in the contested election], there is less certainty about the future orientation of the country, increasingly caught in the crosswind of a new US-Russia power struggle.

In his tour of the region last week [September 2008], [former] US Vice President Dick Cheney shot many salvos against Russians, accusing them of posing a "threat of tyranny, economic blackmail and military invasion" to its neighbors. In his meeting with Aliyev, Cheney was comparatively more reserved and put the emphasis instead on "energy security".

Coinciding with Cheney's trip has been a new report by the European Union's energy commissioner, Andris Piebglas, calling on the EU [European Union] to redouble its efforts to build the US$12 billion Nabucco gas pipeline and reduce its dependence on imports from Russia in the wake of the Georgian crisis that, per a report in the British newspaper *The Guardian*, has led many experts to dismiss the planned 3,300 kilometer Nabucco pipeline from Azerbaijan to Europe via Georgia and Turkey.

> *A top US State Department official has recently called for a strategic, trilateral cooperation between US, Azerbaijan and Turkey.*

Russian and Iranian Resistance

Not only that, both Russia and Iran have opposed the construction of a trans-Caspian pipeline that would allow the shipment of gas from the Caspian section of Turkmenistan to Azerbaijan and then to Europe. Last week, at a meeting of the Caspian littoral states [ones bordering that sea] on the legal status of Caspian Sea, held in Baku, Iran's point man on the Caspian Sea, Mehdi Safari, stated, "We object to the trans-Caspian pipeline because of the possible negative impact on sea ecology. . . . there are Iranian and Russian energy routes and it is unnecessary to jeopardize Caspian ecology".

Although there is real concern about the Caspian ecology, both Tehran and Moscow are equally if not more concerned about the geopolitical ramifications of so-called "pipeline politics" in the Caspian basin and the adjacent regions, particularly now that the US and Europe seem determined to lessen the West's energy dependency on both Iran and Russia by cultivating alternative sources.

The crisis in Georgia is, however, a powerful wake-up call to Baku concerning "roads not taken". On the one hand, Baku is interested in cultivating closer military ties with the West, in light of the Azeri [Azerbaijan's] parliament's recent ratification of an action plan for greater military cooperation with the US. A top US State Department official has recently called for a strategic, trilateral cooperation between US, Azerbaijan and Turkey. And yet, on the other hand, this is precisely the kind of initiative that Baku would be wise to stay away from, unless it is prepared to embrace serious backlashes from its powerful neighbors, Iran and Russia.

One such backlash could conceivably come in the form of Russia's support for the independence of the Azeri breakaway region of Gharabagh, given that the leaders of Upper Gharabagh have welcomed Moscow's decision to recognize the independence of South Ossetia and Abkhazia from Georgia. For now, Moscow is disinclined to back this scenario and Russian Foreign Minister Sergei Lavrov indicated last week that the situation in Gharabagh is "different". That may be small music to Baku's ears, yet few leaders or pundits in Azerbaijan can afford to miss the sobering lesson from the crisis in Georgia, that is, the exorbitant price paid for ignoring Russia's national security concerns.

Maintaining Balance in Foreign Relations

This means that, contrary to some hasty conclusions about "Russia's colossal blunder", to paraphrase *Newsweek*'s Fareed Zakaria, Russia's military gambit in Georgia has not thrown Russia's neighbors in the bosom of the West, but rather, as in the case of Azerbaijan, prompted them to adopt a more cautious foreign policy approach that is geared to maintaining a balance in foreign relations, partly for the sake of protecting fragile borders and territorial integrity. Instead of the North

Atlantic Treaty Organization [NATO], countries such as Georgia and Azerbaijan have the theoretical option of cooperating and or even joining the Shanghai Cooperation Organization, which is dominated by Russia and China. At the moment, this may seem not to be in the cards, yet it makes sense from the prism of regional stability.

In the Caspian Sea, Iran and Russia rely on the existing legal convention for the Caspian that refers to it as a "common sea". That is why both countries are opposed to the division of the Caspian's surface water. The various bilateral and trilateral agreements for the division of the Caspian's underwater resources do not trump the "shared sea" condominium status of the sea that acts as a hinge shutting the door to a foreign presence in the Caspian.

The above means that for the foreseeable future, despite marathon meetings of the five Caspian littoral states, there will most likely not be any new convention, thus guaranteeing the exclusion of NATO or US forces from the important energy hub of the Caspian.

As for Baku's geopolitical orientation, its cordial, business-like relations with Tehran, as well as its pragmatic approach toward the Russia-led geopolitical realities in the region, are prudent courses of action that Baku would be ill-advised to forsake in favor of closer ties with the West. After all, the West has been rather helpless in terms of pulling [the Georgian capital] Tbilisi out of the grave mess that its adventurist leadership carved for itself.

In the Caspian Sea, Iran and Russia rely on the existing legal convention for the Caspian that refers to it as a "common sea".

A Cautious Approach

Concerning the latter, Russian President Dmitry Medvedev has accused the US of providing military assistance to Georgia under the guise of humanitarian assistance. [Former] US Secretary of State Condoleezza Rice, on the other hand, has tried damage-control in US-Russia relations by not putting the kiss of death on the US-Russia nuclear cooperation agreement and, more importantly, not echoing Cheney's blistering verbal volleys.

While we await the results of elections in both the US and Azerbaijan, the latter is likely to thread a cautious middle path that would steer it clear of the headaches gripping the South Caucasus. Needless to say, the pain of such headaches would be much alleviated if Democratic Senator Barack Obama wins in November [of 2008; Obama did win] and somehow succeeds in introducing real change in the hitherto hegemonic orientation of US foreign policy. In that case, the first priority of a president Obama should be to throw water on the new cold war logs fired up by Cheney.

12

A New Cold War Will Not Center on the U.S. and Russia

Mariano Aguirre

Mariano Aguirre is director of the Norwegian Peacebuilding Centre (NOREF) in Oslo. He is a fellow of the Transnational Institute, Amsterdam.

Instead of pitting two superpowers against each other, the new cold war is marked by a multipolarity. America has lost its leading role in global politics, its missile defense system is cause for Russian suspicion, and worries about armed conflicts in the Caucasus and its energy dependency draw Europe into the mix. A new nationalism worldwide is further complicating negotiations between countries. A united Europe has to get involved more deeply, if the many rifts and fault lines in the global political sphere are to be bridged peacefully.

Is there a new Cold War beginning between the United States and Russia? There are signs that would seem to indicate a return of the tension between Moscow and Washington that existed between the end of the Second World War and 1989, based on a contest of military strength and the control of influential regions. The scenario that is emerging now, however, is not one of two ideologically opposed powers competing for the rest of the world. The current one is of two key players within a multipolar international context where various governmental and non-governmental actors fight to advance their own practical interests. In ideological terms, it is no longer

Mariano Aguirre, "A New Cold War or Dangerous Multipolarity?" *Transnational Institute*, May 30, 2007. Reproduced by permission of the author.

about a struggle between communism and capitalism. Now nationalism and other identity-based doctrines are the ideological chips used to gain internal legitimacy—from the messianic patriotism of the United States and Russian nationalistic pride to [Venezuelan President Hugo] Chávez's populism, Chinese neo-communism and the hegemonic nationalism of Iran.

U.S.-Russian Tensions

Speaking at the annual transatlantic conference on security in Munich last February [2007], [former] President Vladimir Putin took advantage of the opportunity to criticize the unilateralism of the United States, George W. Bush's contempt for international law, the Iraq war, and the way in which Washington has approached such issues as support for a possible independent Kosovo and the installation of an antimissile system in Poland and the Czech Republic. All of this, according to the [former] Russian president, has been done without consulting Moscow. Tension between Moscow and Washington has also been raised over what to do in Iran as well as the United States' increasingly aggressive strategy in Afghanistan, which has included pressuring NATO allies to step up troop numbers for offensive action.

NATO's expansion is something that Moscow has been watching uneasily since the 90s when President Bill Clinton failed to include Russia in [the] Alliance's expansion plans.

The United States has proposed that Poland and the Czech Republic form part of a missile system that would, in theory, intercept missiles in the air launched from "rogue states" such as Iran or North Korea. There are several problems with this, however. On one hand, the system is extremely expensive ($225 million has been allocated for next year [2008] alone), and to date it has exhibited nothing but flaws and weaknesses. On the other, Moscow does not see the system as a defence against distant powers but rather as a confirmation, along with the bases that Washington will establish in Romania and Bulgaria, of the encroaching expansion of NATO and the United States to Russia's very borders.

Enclosing Russia

Former Russian Prime Minister Evgueni Primakov wrote last February [2007] in *Moskovskié Novosti* that the idea is to "enclose" Russia and that the appropriate response is to alter Russian military strategy so that it includes the "NATO war machine" among possible threats. In March [2007], *The Guardian* reported that Russian strategy was in the process of being revised, and that the new version would be much tougher on western "expansion" towards "post-Soviet space." That same month, the chairman of the International Affairs Committee of the Russian State Duma stated that, "if the US continues to act unilaterally without giving answers, this could push us towards a crisis. Such a crisis could occur if we stop communicating and start to act unilaterally." The [Russian] Minister of Foreign Affairs has proposed that decisions on Euro-Atlantic security be made using an "integrated approach" in a "trilateral format, including Russia, the EU [European Union] and the US," and that the Russia-NATO Council be used to discuss these issues.

NATO's expansion is something that Moscow has been watching uneasily since the 90s when President Bill Clinton failed to include Russia in [the] Alliance's expansion plans. The former Democrat government's lack of strategy and [George W.] Bush's aggressive unilateralism throughout this decade have acerbated the defensive tendencies of China and Russia. Clinton's strategists began to classify Beijing as a risk for the United States, confusing trade and economic competition with military threat. For the conservative and neoconservative alliance that makes up the Bush administration, having Russia and China as possible strategic and non-democratic adversaries supports their worldview. A view that would seem to be confirmed by the fact that both Moscow and Russia are developing alliances with countries in the [Global] South, as witnessed, for example, by the flow of Chinese investment into Africa or the sale of arms by Russia to Syria and Venezuela.

Ironically, although Cold War ideology is a thing of the past, these mutual perceptions of threat are providing an excuse for re-arming, creating distance and abandoning the international arms control agreements that took so much time and negotiation to reach in previous decades. In 2001, Washington abandoned the ABM (Anti-Ballistic Missiles) Treaty in order to launch its costly system. Moscow is now considering abandoning the 1987 agreement that prevents the deployment of intermediate-range missiles (Intermediate-Range Nuclear Forces Treaty) within Europe. China, for its part, views the United States as an economic competitor with whom there could be military problems, and Russia as an old enemy with whom it must nevertheless maintain a relationship. At the same time, Beijing is also involved in a reconciliation process with Japan. Whatever the case, Beijing believes that re-armament is an essential element in the protection of its economic and trade expansion.

Missile Defense Is a Contentious Issue

Within these power games, Washington, by deploying its anti-missile system in Poland and the Czech Republic, is looking to impose its will on Europe (shades of the Cold War), and is relying on allies such as German Chancellor Angela Merkel and [former] British Prime Minister Tony Blair to counteract any possible criticism from France. In fact, there is a great deal of doubt in Europe about the effectiveness of the antimissile system as well as worry over costs that Europe will be forced to share in the future. However, NATO Secretary General Jaap de Hoop Scheffer is an enthusiastic supporter and has expressed his desire that NATO re-armament plans be coordinated with those of Washington, especially since the antimissile system will not cover countries in Southern Europe. Such coordination would prevent differences within the Alliance.

Indeed, the debate over the installation of a new missile system is beginning to generate tension in Europe. The German coalition government is divided on the installation of the antimissile system in Eastern Europe: while Merkel completely agrees with it (although she has suggested that Washington should consult Moscow more often), Foreign Minister Frank-Walter Steinmeier has come out against it, as has the leader of the Social Democratic party (SPD), Kurt Beck.

The United States is no longer the dominating global power.

A New Superpower

After almost a decade of crisis and weakness, Russia is depending upon the authoritarian centralization of power and, more particularly, on oil revenues and nuclear arms to boost its influence and regain the power it enjoyed during the Cold War. With the 2008 elections just around the corner, Putin is taking a strong stance on the West in order to win over domestic nationalists and gain the support of the Russian military. At the same time, Russia wants to be seen as a powerful nation once again, one that cannot be questioned on its domestic policies whether they are restrictions on freedom of expression or business, or repressive military intervention in Chechnya.

As Dmitri Trenin, Deputy Director of the Carnegie Moscow Center, explains it, "The Kremlin's new approach to foreign policy assumes that as a big country, Russia is essentially friendless; no great power wants a strong Russia, which would be a formidable competitor, and many want a weak Russia that they could exploit and manipulate. Accordingly, Russia has a choice between accepting subservience and reasserting its status as a great power, thereby claiming its rightful place in the world alongside the United States and China rather than settling for the company of Brazil and India."

Europe seems to be at the centre of these tensions but in fact the whole international system is in a process of deep change. The United States is no longer the dominating global power. Although still powerful, it has serious domestic problems, has lost international credibility and suffers from a lack of strategic vision, all of which have caused it to lose its leadership role. The European Union hopes that Washington will regain its leadership in the post-Bush era, although it may have to accept the need to act alone, without waiting for the United States. China and Russia are emerging from the post-Cold War transition period as powers with strong regional and, in the case of Beijing, global influence. Likewise, India, Brazil and South Africa have achieved significant regional power.

The greatest danger is that this fragmentation of power is, in many cases, moving towards a nationalism based on practical interests, more conservative than cooperative in nature, with each country defending its own interests, rather than moving towards a cooperative multilateral system. Hence, it is moving towards a dangerous multipolarity. Eventually, Europe may be the only multi-state alliance whose union is based on a common will, shared security norms and cooperative policies, including a foreign policy that reflects this way of relating to the world. This, however, makes it all the more urgent for Europe to take a more coherent and proactive stance.

13

The New Cold War Is with Iran

Thomas Friedman

Thomas Friedman is a Pulitzer Prize-winning commentator for the New York Times.

The new cold war pits America against Iran, not Russia. Iran has outsmarted America in the Middle East and has become a formidable force. Despite Iran's providing support to many militias in the Middle East and seeking nuclear energy, the West won't be able to attack, because it could lead to fighting throughout the region. America has neither the respect nor the leverage to implement its policies and can't protect its friends from attacks.

The next American president will inherit many foreign policy challenges, but surely one of the biggest will be the Cold War. Yes, the next U.S. president is going to be a Cold War president—but this Cold War is with Iran.

That is the real umbrella story in the Middle East today— the struggle for influence across the region, with America and its Sunni Arab allies (and Israel) versus Iran, Syria and their nonstate allies, Hamas and Hezbollah. As the May 11 editorial in the Iranian daily Kayhan put it, "In the power struggle in the Middle East, there are only two sides: Iran and the U.S."

For now, Team America is losing on just about every front. How come? The short answer is that Iran is smart and ruthless, America is dumb and weak, and the Sunni Arab world is feckless and divided. Any other questions?

The outrage of the week is the Iranian-Syrian-Hezbollah attempt to take over Lebanon. Hezbollah thugs pushed into Sunni neighborhoods in West Beirut, focusing particular attention on crushing progressive news outlets like Future TV, so Hezbollah's propaganda machine could dominate the airwaves. The Shiite militia Hezbollah emerged supposedly to protect Lebanon from Israel. Having done that, it has now turned around and sold Lebanon to Syria and Iran.

All of this is part of what Ehud Yaari, one of Israel's best Middle East watchers, calls "Pax Iranica." In his April 28 column in *The Jerusalem Report*, Yaari pointed out the web of influence that Iran has built around the Middle East—from the sway it has over Iraq's prime minister, Nuri Kamal al-Maliki, to its ability to manipulate virtually all the Shiite militias in Iraq, to its building up of Hezbollah into a force—with 40,000 rockets—that can control Lebanon and threaten Israel should it think of striking Tehran, to its ability to strengthen Hamas in Gaza and block any U.S.-sponsored Israeli-Palestinian peace.

For now, Team America is losing on just about every front.

"Simply put," noted Yaari, "Tehran has created a situation in which anyone who wants to attack its atomic facilities will have to take into account that this will lead to bitter fighting" on the Lebanese, Palestinian, Iraqi and Persian Gulf fronts. That is a sophisticated strategy of deterrence.

The Bush team, by contrast, in eight years has managed to put America in the unique position in the Middle East where it is "not liked, not feared and not respected," writes Aaron David Miller, a former Mideast negotiator under both Republican and Democratic administrations, in his provocative new book on the peace process, titled *The Much Too Promised Land*.

"We stumbled for eight years under Bill Clinton over how to make peace in the Middle East, and then we stumbled for eight years under George Bush over how to make war there," said Miller, and the result is "an America that is trapped in a region which it cannot fix and it cannot abandon."

Look at the last few months, he said: Bush went to the Middle East in January, Secretary of State Condoleezza Rice went in February, Vice President Dick Cheney went in March, the secretary of state went again in April, and the president is there again this week. After all that, oil prices are as high as ever and peace prospects as low as ever. As Miller puts it, America right now "cannot defeat, co-opt or contain" any of the key players in the region.

We Americans are not going to war with Iran, nor should we.

The big debate between Barack Obama and Hillary Clinton is over whether or not the United States should talk to Iran. Obama is in favor; Clinton has been against. Alas, the right question for the next president isn't whether we talk or don't talk. It's whether we have leverage or don't have leverage.

When you have leverage, talk. When you don't have leverage, get some—by creating economic, diplomatic or military incentives and pressures that the other side finds too tempting or frightening to ignore. That is where the Bush team has been so incompetent vis-a-vis Iran.

The only weaker party is the Sunni Arab world, which is either so drunk on oil it thinks it can buy its way out of any Iranian challenge or is so divided it can't make a fist to protect its own interests—or both. We Americans are not going to war with Iran, nor should we. But it is sad to see America and its Arab friends so weak they can't prevent one of the last corners of decency, pluralism and openness in the Arab world from being snuffed out by Iran and Syria. The only thing that gives me succor is the knowledge that anyone who has ever tried to dominate Lebanon alone—Maronites, Palestinians, Syrians, Israelis—has triggered a backlash and failed.

"Lebanon is not a place anyone can control without a consensus, without bringing everybody in," said the Lebanese columnist Michael Young. "Lebanon has been a graveyard for people with grand projects." In the Middle East, he added, your enemies always seem to "find a way of joining together and suddenly making things very difficult for you."

14

China Might Be Opposing U.S. in a New Cold War

Emanuel Pastreich

Emanuel Pastreich serves as Director of the Asia Institute at the Solbridge School of Business in Daejeon, South Korea.

Many observers believe that another rivalry mirroring the Cold War could arise between America and China. Yet this rivalry should play out as an economic and cultural one, rather than an armed conflict. America has lost its economic dominance and is mired in wars and scandals, leaving room for China to emerge as a serious player on the global stage. Only if America forfeits diplomacy and common sense could the specter of a military confrontation become reality.

There was nothing surprising about Bill Gertz's inflammatory article in the Feb. 15 [2006] *Washington Times* speculating about "secret underground arms facilities" in China. The drive to paint China as a threat akin to the Soviet Union in the American mind serves those corporate interests that manufacture weapons systems while obscuring the true nature of the predicament in which [the] United States finds itself.

The implied analogy between the Soviet Union of the 1960s and the People's Republic of China today found in such journalism may serve to prop up an obsolete Cold War security system that refuses to adjust to the true dangers of a globalized world, but it does so by diverting attention from the palpable challenge that China poses for the United States.

Emanuel Pastreich, "Is China the Nemesis in a New Cold War?" *Nautilus Institute,* March 6, 2006. Reproduced by permission. www.nautilus.org.

The relationship between the United States and the People's Republic of China today bears a far greater similarity to the bitter rivalry between Great Britain and the United States that played out between 1910 and 1970. That contest, although obscured by contemporary ideology positing Great Britain as America's closest ally, was not a military conflict, but rather a global struggle over markets, finance, technology and cultural authority. Unfortunately, after winning that contest decisively in the last century, the United States is blithely walking down the same path that England did in the previous century, but at a faster pace.

History Is Repeating Itself

Great Britain maintained undisputed dominion in the economic, diplomatic and military realms at the start of the [20]th century. Although England had its rivals, the British navy controlled the shipping lanes, the British Sterling served as the universal currency, English culture carried awesome authority, and the sun never set on the Empire.

As Britain's rival for global domination, the U.S. did not offer military confrontation with Britain, even as it increased the size of its military considerably. Rather, the U.S. calmly set to work in other areas, ultimately supplanting Great Britain as the dominant political, social, and economic world power.

Great Britain actually helped the U.S. in that process much as the U.S. aids China today. Britain's ensnarement in two debilitating world wars during the 20th century taxed its resources to the limit and encouraged reliance on the United States for both finance and manufacturing. For example, during the Second World War, it was not that the United States forcibly took control of shipping lanes from England, but rather the U.S. Navy stepped in to protect shipping lanes when the British Navy proved, due to overextension and other commitments, unequal to the task.

It requires no stretch of the imagination to envision a scenario in which the United States concedes its dominant status to China, not because of China's nuclear arsenal, but rather because the U.S. has unnecessarily mired itself in a global "War on Terror" that, because the term "terror" is so broad in meaning, recognizes no end and promises to harm America's prosperity, curtail its traditional freedoms, and leave a moral blot on its reputation among the community of nations.

Americans can no longer completely ignore the amount of American debt that the People's Republic of China has bought up.

A Shift of Power

The 20th century also saw the United States increase, gradually but decisively, its control of technology, intellectual capital, and market share. Although Great Britain did not fully appreciate the rise in American sophistication, over time England found itself crucially dependent upon American support. Before the First World War, England was the primary source for capital, controlling over 40 percent of overseas investments. After that war, however, England found itself deeply in debt, mostly to the United States. As a consequence, interest payments soaked up almost 40 percent of British government expenditures thereafter.

World War II allowed England to dig itself into an even deeper pit. For example, the Lend-Lease program supplying England with war materiel at the height of the conflict required that British production be dedicated to the war effort, rather than to goods for export. The predictable result was that overall British exports in 1944 were 31 percent of what they had been in 1938. If the analogy to the Lend-Lease Program seems farfetched to readers, that is in part because the role of Chinese manufacturing in supporting the present American military campaign is so poorly understood.

Similarly, the American debt to China, and other Asian nations, is often dismissed by economists who cite the unique position of the Dollar in the world economy. But is there any good reason to assume that the Dollar will not, over time, ultimately follow the path of the British Sterling? Americans can no longer completely ignore the amount of American debt that the People's Republic of China has bought up. China has also made deep inroads in the fields of high technology and manufacturing at the start of this century as the U.S. did at the dawn of the last one. Although Americans may comfort themselves with the assumption that China still does not possess the most advanced technology, the technological gap between the U.S. and China has shrunk considerably in many fields. Moreover, although it is true that China would suffer considerably from a downturn in the American economy, the undeniable fact is that China is diversifying its markets whereas the United States is concentrating its debt.

There will always be the possibility of a military conflict between the United States and the People's Republic of China.

China Has Become a Popular Partner

Even in ideological terms, the rivalry between the United States and China displays striking parallels to that between England and the United States in the previous century. China has studiously avoided statements about a moral imperative to interfere in the affairs of other nations at the very moment that the United States makes constant calls for the opening of markets, the importance of democracy and the dangers of terrorism. American insistence on this narrow agenda has benefited China immensely. Because the Chinese expand economic ties throughout the world without passing judgment on other nations, they have become popular partners for many in marked contrast to the demanding Americans.

The Chinese approach recalls the Open Door policy for trade advocated by the United States in the 19th century and the ideal of "self-determination" pronounced by President Woodrow Wilson in the twentieth. The United States slowly tipped perception on a global scale by presenting itself as a nation concerned with the sovereignty of the peoples of the world—in contrast to Great Britain's pride in its colonial empire. Most nations today see American demands as a direct violation of their sovereignty and therefore find in China an easier negotiating partner.

The Specter of Armed Confrontation

Of course there will always be the possibility of a military conflict between the United States and the People's Republic of China. Even American security planners sympathetic to China are aware of that scenario—and plan for it. But intentional misdiagnosis of the challenge posed by China is far more dangerous for the U.S. in the long run. Posing the threat in purely military terms allows Americans to deny the negative trends in technology and economics bedeviling the United States. If a serious response to that threat is put off, the day will come when it no longer can be remedied.

Finally, arguments about a military threat from China make clear just how narrow America's responses have become. The United States is losing its economic and cultural authority through the lethal mixture of ballooning trade deficits and torture scandals. The danger is that a classic military reflex will be one of the few tools left in the chest at a time when the U.S. needs a far more varied and sophisticated set of responses to negotiate successfully the path ahead. The image of China as an ominous rising military power serves the purpose of drawing attention away from the degree to which the American military has been gutted in the name of privatization, leaving basic facilities neglected as an increasingly fragmented and unfocused conflict is pursued. Planning for a global confrontation with China may help maintain the status quo and prop up an outmoded security system, but it does so at the very moment that the United States is approaching the absolute limits of its material power.

15

Africa Might Become the Staging Ground of a New Cold War with China

Christopher Moraff

Christopher Moraff is a journalist and photographer and a frequent contributor to the magazines In These Times, *the* American Prospect Online, *and* Common Sense.

Africa has long been a forgotten continent, but in recent years, both the U.S. and China have stepped up their efforts to open to new markets for their economies and gain political influence on the continent. Partly driven by the desire to secure energy resources, the countries' initiatives could lead to a standoff on African soil, and create tensions that might lead to a new cold war.

The forgotten continent of Africa could become the new battleground in the next American conflict.

On Feb. 6 [2007], President [George W.] Bush formally established the U.S. Africa Command (AFRICOM), a unified command structure located on the continent. By 2012, the United States wants two dozen bases in Africa to promote U.S. security interests and "the common goals of development of health, education, democracy, and economic growth."

Bush announced the creation of AFRICOM a week after Chinese President Hu Jintao landed in Cameroon to start a high-profile, eight-country African tour, during which he signed more than 50 cooperation agreements and pledged to double China's assistance to Africa by 2009.

New U.S. Strategic Interests

Despite a surge in interest during the Cold War, Africa has never played a strategic role in U.S. foreign policy. In 1995, the Department of Defense stated: "Ultimately we see very little traditional strategic interest in Africa." But with increasing investment from an energy-hungry China, the United States is reconsidering.

"It's an ideological game," says Vijay Prashad, director of international studies at Trinity College. "Since China began to enter Africa with a new development agenda, it called the United States' bluff. Now Africa is becoming the battlefield of ideas over two forms of hegemony."

According to the State Department, Chinese trade with Africa quadrupled to $55 billion from 2002 to 2006. China estimates there are 800 Chinese firms investing in Africa.

Neoconservative groups call China's growing relationship with Africa "alarming" and want a response. "The United States must be alert to the potential long-term disruption of American access to important raw materials and energy sources as these resources are 'locked up' by Chinese firms," reads a 2006 Heritage Foundation policy backgrounder.

While many NGOs [nongovernmental organizations] have joined U.S. lawmakers in supporting AFRICOM in principle, there is skepticism.

In recent testimony on Capitol Hill, Mark Malan, a program officer with Refugees International, summed up the NGO position: "The main concern of operational NGOs is that AFRICOM will increase the trend towards the militarization of humanitarian action, which raises fundamental concerns about the purpose of such assistance."

Some critics see AFRICOM as another foothold for the military-industrial complex. "AFRICOM ... reflects the

[George W.] Bush administration's primary reliance on the use of force to pursue its strategic interests," writes Salim Lone, a former spokesman for the U.N. mission in Iraq and a columnist with the *Daily Nation* in Nairobi.

The National Intelligence Council projects that African oil imports could account for 25 percent of total U.S. imports by 2015.

The Goal Remains Unclear

U.S. officials have stated what AFRICOM will not do—"this *isn't* about chasing terrorists around Africa"; "AFRICOM *isn't* going to be used to protect natural resources"; "AFRICOM will in *no way* take a leadership role in the area of diplomacy." Exactly what it *will* do is unclear.

But that hasn't stopped AFRICOM from garnering support at home—even from progressives such as Sen. Russ Feingold (D-Wisc.). His House counterpart, Rep. Donald Payne (D-N.J.), is more skeptical. "To the extent that establishing a command where our relationship with Africa is the priority rather than an afterthought can do so, I support it," said Payne, who chairs the Subcommittee on Africa & Global Health. "However, I do have some serious concerns."

Others say the Defense Department must tread carefully. "It's not that the idea itself is bad when you look at some of the things that have happened there, but we need to be very artful in how we proceed," said a high-ranking Democratic staffer. "This administration has not made it easy for the U.S. to seem credible on security issues. The current environment doesn't really leave room for error."

Regardless, Africa's mounting importance as a global petroleum source cannot be underestimated. Since 2002, U.S. oil imports from Nigeria, Angola, Algeria and Libya have nearly doubled, and according to data from the Energy Information

Administration, Africa has surpassed the Middle East as the largest supplier of crude oil to the United States. The National Intelligence Council projects that African oil imports could account for 25 percent of total U.S. imports by 2015. At the same time, China accounted for 40 percent of total growth in global demand for oil in the last four years. Today, more than a quarter of China's oil imports come from Africa.

That demand indicates Africa will begin to play a much larger role in both U.S. and Chinese foreign policy over the coming decades, as the large powers play yet another round of the age-old "great game."

Organizations to Contact

The editors have compiled the following list of organizations concerned with the issues debated in this book. The descriptions are derived from materials provided by the organizations. All have publications or information available for interested readers. The list was compiled on the date of publication of the present volume; the information provided here may change. Be aware that many organizations take several weeks or longer to respond to inquiries, so allow as much time as possible.

The Brookings Institute
1775 Massachusetts Ave. NW, Washington, DC   20036
(202) 797-6000 • fax: (202) 797-6004
e-mail: brookinfo@brook.edu
Web site: www.brookings.org

The Brookings Institute is a think tank conducting research and education in foreign policy, economics, government, and the social sciences. Publications include the quarterly *Brookings Review*, periodic *Policy Briefs*, and books including *Terrorism and U.S. Foreign Policy*.

Center for Defense Information (CDI)
1779 Massachusetts Ave. NW, Suite 615
Washington, DC   20036
(202) 332-0600 • fax: (202) 462-4559
e-mail: info@cdi.org
Web site: www.cdi.org

CDI is a nonpartisan, nonprofit organization that researches all aspects of global security. It seeks to educate the public and policy makers about weapons systems, security policy, and defense budgeting. It publishes the monthly *Defense Monitor*.

Center for Strategic and International Studies (CSIS)
1800 K Street NW, Suite 400, Washington, DC   20006
(202) 887-0200 • fax: (202) 775-3199
Web site: http://csis.org

The center works to provide world leaders with strategic insights and policy options on current and emerging global issues. It publishes the *Washington Quarterly*, a journal on political, economic, and security issues, and other publications that can be downloaded from its Web site.

Central Intelligence Agency (CIA)
Office of Public Affairs, Washington, DC   20505
(703) 482-0623 • fax: (703) 482-1739
Web site: www.cia.gov

The Central Intelligence Agency was created in 1947 with the signing of the National Security Act by President Harry S. Truman. The CIA seeks to collect and evaluate intelligence related to national security and provide appropriate dissemination of such intelligence. Publications such as the *Factbook on Intelligence* are available on its Web site.

Foreign Policy Association (FPA)
470 Park Avenue South, New York, NY   10016
(212) 481-8100 • fax: (212) 481-9275
e-mail: info@fpa.org
Web site: www.fpa.org

The FPA is a nonprofit organization seeking to inspire the American public to learn more about the world. The FPA serves as a catalyst for developing awareness, understanding of, and providing informed opinions on global issues. It publishes the *Great Decisions* DVD series, and makes articles and discussions available online.

The Heritage Foundation
214 Massachusetts Ave. NE, Washington, DC   20002-4999
(202) 546-4400 • fax: (202) 546-8328

e-mail: info@heritage.org
Web site: www.heritage.org

Founded in 1973, The Heritage Foundation is a research and educational institute, whose mission is to formulate and promote conservative public policies based on the principles of free enterprise, limited government, individual freedom, and a strong national defense. It publishes many books on foreign policy, such as *Winning the Long War*.

Institute for Policy Studies (IPS)
1112 16th Street NW, Suite 600, Washington, DC   20036
(202) 234-9382 • fax: (202) 387-7915
Web site: www.ips-dc.org

The IPS is a progressive think tank working to develop societies built around the values of justice and nonviolence. It publishes reports including *Global Perspectives: A Media Guide to Foreign Policy Experts*. Articles are also available online.

National Security Agency (NSA)
9800 Savage Road, Fort Meade, MD   20755-6248
(301) 688-6524
Web site: www.nsa.gov

The NSA coordinates, directs, and performs activities, such as designing cipher systems, which protect American information systems and produce foreign intelligence information. Speeches, briefings, and reports are available online.

Bibliography

Books

Yonah Alexander and Milton Hoenig *The New Iranian Leadership: Ahmadinejad, Terrorism, Nuclear Ambition, and the Middle East.* Santa Barbara, CA: Greenwood Publishing Group, 2007.

Ali Ansari *Iran Under Ahmadinejad.* New York, NY: Routledge, 2008.

David J. Betz *Civil-Military Relations in Russia and Eastern Europe.* New York, NY: Routledge, 2004.

Jonathan Brent *Inside the Stalin Archives: Discovering the New Russia.* New York, NY: Atlas & Co., 2008.

Zbigniew Brzezinski, Robert Gates, and Suzanne Maloney *Iran: Time for a New Approach.* Council on Foreign Relations Press, 2004.

Janusz Bugajski *Toward an Understanding of Russia: New European Perspectives.* Council on Foreign Relations Press, 2002.

Hannah Carter and Anoushiravan Ehteshami *The Middle East's Relations with Asia and Russia.* New York, NY: RoutledgeCurzon, 2004.

Padma Desai *Conversations on Russia: Reform from Yeltsin to Putin.* New York, NY: Oxford University Press, 2006.

Ben Eklof,
Larry Holmes,
and Vera Kaplan

Educational Reform in Post-Soviet Russia: Legacies and Prospects. London, UK: Frank Cass, 2005.

Marshall
Goldman

Petrostate: Putin, Power, and the New Russia. New York, NY: Oxford University Press, 2008.

Gabriel
Gorodetsky

Russia between East and West: Russian Foreign Policy on the Threshold of the Twenty-First Century. London, UK: Frank Cass, 2003.

Mark Hitchcock

The Apocalypse of Ahmadinejad: The Revelation of Iran's Nuclear Prophet. Portland, OR: Multnomah Publications, 2007.

Alireza Jafarzadeh

The Iran Threat: President Ahmadinejad and the Coming Nuclear Crisis. New York, NY: Palgrave Macmillan, 2007.

Boris Kagarlitsky

Russia Under Yeltsin and Putin: Neo-Liberal Autocracy. London, UK: Pluto Press, 2002.

Dianne Kirby, ed.

Religion and the Cold War. New York, NY: Palgrave Macmillan, 2002.

Steve LeVine

Putin's Labyrinth: Spies, Murder, and the Dark Heart of the New Russia. New York, NY: Random House, 2008.

Edward Lucas

The New Cold War: Putin's Russia and the Threat to the West. New York, NY: MacMillan, 2009.

Mark MacKinnon — *The New Cold War: Revolutions, Rigged Elections and Pipeline Politics in the Former Soviet Union*. Toronto, ON: Random House Canada, 2007.

Yossi Melman and Meir Javedanfar — *The Nuclear Sphinx of Tehran: Mahmoud Ahmadinejad and the State of Iran*. New York, NY: Basic Books, 2008.

Kasra Naji — *Ahmadinejad: The Secret History of Iran's Radical Leader*. Berkeley, CA: University of California Press, 2008.

Thomas Parland — *The Extreme Nationalist Threat in Russia: The Growing Influence of Western Rightist Ideas*. New York, NY: RoutledgeCurzon, 2004.

Scott Ritter — *Target Iran: The Truth about the U.S. Government's Plans for Regime Change*. Australia: Allen & Unwin, 2006.

Neil Robinson — *Russia: A State of Uncertainty*. New York, NY: Routledge, 2002.

Richard Rose and Neil Munro — *Elections Without Order: Russia's Challenge to Vladimir Putin*. Cambridge University Press, 2002.

Richard Sakwa — *Putin: Russia's Choice*. 2nd ed. Abingdon, Oxfordshire: Routledge, 2008.

Anton Steen — *Political Elites and the New Russia: The Power Basis of Yeltsin's and Putin's Regimes*. New York, NY: Routledge/Curzon, 2003.

Mikhail Stoliarov   *Federalism and the Dictatorship of Power in Russia.* New York, NY: Routledge, 2003.

Peter Truscott   *Putin's Progress: A Biography of Russia's Enigmatic President, Vladimir Putin.* London: Simon & Schuster Ltd., 2004.

Periodicals

Anders Aslund   "The Hunt for Russia's Riches: Clamping Down on Oligarchs Has Been at the Top of Vladimir Putin's To-Do List, But His Authoritarian Agenda Is Holding Russia Back. As Much as Putin May Resent the Country's Wealthy Elite, Russia Needs Them to Service," *Foreign Policy,* January 2006.

Associated Press   "Canada to Claim Arctic Passage," *Washington Times,* August 20, 2007.

Peter Baker   "U.S.-Russia Relations Chilly Amid Transition," *Washington Post,* March 1, 2008.

Bertrand Benoit   "US Missile Shield Plan Draws Fire in Germany," *Financial Times,* April 9, 2007.

Samuel Berger   "Talk to Tehran," *Wall Street Journal,* May 8, 2006.

Joseph Biden, Jr.   "After Putin," *Wall Street Journal,* March 24, 2008.

Ed Blanche   "Back to the Future: Russian Navy Discussions About the Possibilities of Restoring Bases in Syria in Order to Bolster Moscow's Drive to Regain Its Influence in the Middle East Have Led to Speculation about the Start of a New Cold War," *Middle East*, October 2007.

Ed Blanche   "From Russia 'With Love': Russia's President Putin Declares War on Jihadists after Moscow's Diplomats Are Kidnapped and Killed in Iraq," *Middle East*, August 2006.

Colin Brown   "A Good Day to Bury the Bad News That Ministerial Car Use Has Soared," *Independent*, July 27, 2007.

Stephen Cohen   "The Media's New Cold War: Ukraine's Contested Election Was a Call to Arms for America's Punditry," *Nation*, January 31, 2005.

Daniel Dombey   "NATO Warns US Missiles May Divide Europe," *Financial Times*, March 12, 2007.

Taylor Downing   "Under the Mushroom Cloud: The Cold War Has Become This Year's Hot Media Topic. Taylor Downing Welcomes the Chance to Look More Critically at the Era of 'Mutually Assured Destruction,'" *History Today*, August 2008.

Joschka Fischer   "The Case for Bargaining With Iran," *Washington Post*, May 29, 2006.

Misha Glenny   "Gas & Gangsters: Energy Is the Key
                   to Europe's New Relationship with
                   Russia—And Supposedly Moscow's
                   Weapon of Choice in Its Plan for
                   European Domination. Yet This New
                   Cold War Is Not Inevitable," *New
                   Statesman*, February 28, 2008.

Luke Harding   "The New Cold War: Russia's
                   Missiles to Target Europe," *Guardian*,
                   June 4, 2007.

Luke Harding   "Russian Generals Aim Again at
                   NATO and the West," *Guardian
                   Weekly*, March 16, 2007.

Luke Harding   "Russian Missile Test Adds to Arms
                   Race Fears," *Guardian*, May 30, 2007.

Michael Hoffman   "Army General to Direct Missile
                   Defense Agency," *Army Times*, March
                   20, 2008.

William Jasper   "Putin, Poison, and Murder: The
                   Recent Murder-by-Poison of Russian
                   KGB/FSB Defector Alexander
                   Litvinenko Is a Potent Warning about
                   the Dangers of Our New Security
                   'Partnership' with Putin's Russia,"
                   New American, January 22, 2007.

Fred Kaplan   "Whose Missile Shield Is It,
                   Anyway?" Slate.com, May 23, 2006.

Henry Kissinger   "A Nuclear Test for Diplomacy,"
                   Washington Post, May 16, 2006.

Konstantin Kosachev
"America and Russia: From Cold War to Cold Shoulder," *Financial Times*, March 23, 2007.

Sergei Lavrov
"A Crucial Debate on Europe's Anti-Missile Defences," *Financial Times*, April 11, 2007.

Benjamin Maack
"The Cold War's Missing Atom Bombs," *Der Spiegel*, November 14, 2008.

David Zane Mairowitz
"Outpost of the New Cold War," *Progressive*, April 2004.

Steven Lee Myers
"No Cold War, Perhaps, but Surely a Lukewarm Peace," *New York Times*, February 18, 2007.

Sam Nunn
"Nuclear Pig in a Poke," *Wall Street Journal*, May 24, 2006.

Eric Posner
"The New Race for the Arctic," *Wall Street Journal*, August 3, 2007.

Peter Spiegel
"Pentagon Chief Talks Tough on Russia," *Los Angeles Times*, March 17, 2008.

Dmitri Trenin
"Russia Leaves the West," *Foreign Affairs*, July–August, 2006.

Eric Umansky
"Lost Over Iran," *Columbia Journalism Review*, March/April 2008.

Patrick Wintour
"Putin Surprises US with Missile Suggestion," *Guardian*, June 8, 2007.

Index